From Trench to Sky

Letters Home 1915 – 1918

from

Arthur George "Jolly Pierre" Wilson

Transcribed, notated and compiled by

Michael Wilson

"We will remember them",
With best wishes,
God Bless,

Michael A. Wilson   Oct. 2008.

ISBN 978-1-904499-22-0

Further copies of this book may be obtained from

Roundtuit Publishing
32 Cookes Wood
Broom Park
Durham DH7 7RL
email: orders@roundtuitpublishing
07980 920 078

First published in UK in 2008 by Roundtuit Publishing,
32 Cookes Wood, Broom Park, Durham DH7 7RL.

Printed in the United Kingdom of Great Britain by Prontaprint Greenock 0845 130 7708

Front Cover: Photographs of "Jolly Pierre", soldier in trenches, Peter and friends with Bristol Fighter, a letter home and a page from Peter's flight log

Dedication

To all those valiant young men and women who sacrificed their
lives or their mental or physical health
in the Great Wars and who, thus, had no future to build,

nor dreams to fulfil.

Watercolour given to my father by the artist Eric Kennington

In grateful appreciation of the splendid work done by Combat Stress and Erskine (Renfrew)*in caring for our ex-service men and women I propose giving £1.00 to each of these very worthy charities from each book sold or presented.   MICHAEL A WILSON

*

3

Contents

List of Illustrations

Acknowledgements

I would like to pay tribute to my dear wife, Rosemary, for her forbearance during the long months it has taken me to edit and compile this little book. The dining room has been littered with boxes of papers, photographs and letters. She has also given wise counsel as to which parts of the letters could be omitted to avoid too much repetition. As she says "it has been a long, painful gestation period". Put that down to my garden and to my soon-to-be octogenarian status!!

I am also grateful to friends and family who have encouraged me to print these letters for the sake of posterity. When I was still pondering, Christopher Guise, Frances Westley and Ted Denison (former Hon. Colonel 3rd Battalion T.A. Prince of Wales's Own Regiment) urged me to go ahead just when my resolution was faltering. Jill Campbell has done all the typing and showed infinite patience in deciphering the original letters and dealing with my tinkering. We have been been aided by her husband, Colin, whose wizardry with his computer has been a great help.

Finally, I must mention the photographs. I have felt very strongly that for new generations to understand the awful conditions described in the letters, and to depict the general scene in France and Flanders, it was essential to include some photographs. I have used some from my father's collection, many have been provided by the Prince of Wales's Own Regiment of Yorkshire Museum in York where Graham Dyson, the Assistant Curator, was of special assistance. Others, very useful for setting the scene, have come from my father's treasured collection of The War Illustrated ("A Pictorial Record of the Conflict of the Nations" edited by J. A. Hammerton) from 1914-1918. Victoria Watkins drew the map for me.

The photograph of an RE8 preparing for a night mission on page 92 is shown courtesy of The Photograph Archive at the Imperial War Museum.

A late but essential acknowledgement must go to the printers whom I have recently found across the water in Greenock. Philip Wilson (a school friend of my son Alistair) and his enthusiastic team at Prontaprint are being splendid. And thanks to Phil I have been put in contact with Nancy Radford of Roundtuit Publishing in Durham whose experience is proving invaluable as we enter the home straight. Her ideas, and willingness to help with the publishing and distribution, are taking a big load off my ancient shoulders. I hope she won't mind being called a "treasure"!

I would like to thank Barbara Littlejohn, the artist's daughter, for permission to include the Bruce Bairnsfather's drawing on page 58.

Michael A Wilson, Cardross, January 2008

Introduction

In 2005 a remarkable thing happened. Was meant to happen! Thanks to the diligence of a police inspector in Maida Vale, a treasure trove of letters written by my father 90 years ago, has been returned to the family. They were nearly all written from the Front line in Flanders in 1915 and were in the bottom of an ancient portmanteau containing sundry music books, school reports and letters offering no clue as to ownership. It was some months before the portmanteau finally reached me in Scotland and several more months elapsed before I worked my way to the bottom of what appeared to be a fairly hum-drum collection of an old lady's treasures. Imagine my pleasure when a little bundle of letters in my father's handwriting was the final item to appear at the very bottom of the case! And then a sense of astonishment and joy when I realised that these precious letters had actually been written from the front line in 1915.

The owner of the deed box, my aunt Barbara, died in 1983, and the house to which the letters were addressed is now the site of a supermarket in a Yorkshire village. There was only one clue: a letter written by me to the late Canon Harry Broughton, the widower of my aunt, on the occasion of the death of my father in 1990.

I do not care how the case fell into the hands of the police. I am certain that my father wished me to see these remarkable letters, and to make them available to the family and to anyone else who might find them of interest from an historical or social history point of view. It is curiously relevant that my father's great grandchildren are now studying World War One as history.

Having started to sort out the letters (they were in quite a muddle) I realised that due to censorship, they could only tell part of Peter's story. It dawned on me that I could make Peter's World War One experiences much more comprehensive for any readers, if I could set them in the context of a broader account of Peter's experiences with the West Yorkshire Regiment (1914-1917) and later with the R.F.C., in France and Belgium. Luckily I had a helpful source at hand as a consequence of having persuaded my father to write down some of his memories of a full life, when he was in a retirement home in his nineties. I believe readers will find it helpful if I include a few extracts from a book about these memories, which I published in 1993. These extracts from his memoirs and diaries are printed in italics for clarity of reference.

I trust readers will pardon me for having included the full text of many of the letters. Inevitably there is a lot of repetition in the salutations to his family and friends and references to the remarkable and steady stream of food parcels which somehow found their way to him at the front, but I feel they should be included as an indication of the family ties and support which kept those valiant young men of the B.E.F. going in such appalling conditions. I have, however, trimmed some of the references to family, friends and food parcels in later letters.

The other factor which shines through nearly every page of these letters is the unshakeable faith in his God, which sustained him in those terrible trenches. A friend has commented "The letters are a remarkable testimony of a 20 year old, which unlike much other material from the 1914-1918 war, shed light on how a person with a background of strong faith managed to cope with the horrors of it all". That comment strengthened my resolve to include the remarkably apt verses from the Bible with which he started nearly every letter, and to include the many other passages in the letters in which he refers to his trust in the good Lord to watch over him. Peter's story would not be complete without them. Please ponder how much his Christian faith, forged in his home, in Sunday School in the village of Haxby, and at school in St Peter's, York, helped him through tough times. Again in later letters I have done a little trimming, though you might not think so!

The letters were written in pencil, most six or more pages long. The different types of paper used helped me to join up letters which had become scattered.

I do hope you will find this little book a worthy companion to dip into from time to time. I would like to think that Jolly Pierre's testimony might help and encourage you when times are difficult.

The Wilson family in the garden of Ashtree House, Haxby about 1901. Peter seated centre.

Prologue

My father was christened Arthur George but from an early age he was "Peter" to friends and family. It seems that his resilience and contagious optimism, in even the most awful situations, led him to be nicknamed "Jolly Pierre" by his comrades-in-arms. Hence the title of this little book.

The family consisted of his father, also Arthur George, whom he usually addressed as "Pater", his mother Barbara Annie, his two sisters, Barbara and Mary, and his younger brother Edward. The home also gave shelter to his mother's widowed sister, Mary Elizabeth, and her daughter Florence ("Flopsy"). They lived in Ashtree House in the village of Haxby near York.

My father left school (St Peter's, York) in 1912 and worked in Becketts Bank in Knaresborough. Early in 1914 he volunteered for the Territorial Army and joined the West Yorkshire Regiment in Knaresborough. He was training under canvas on August 4th, when war was declared.

In April 1915 his regiment, the 5th West Yorks, was posted to France to join the B.E.F. and took part in the fierce battle of Aubers Ridge in May 1915. Thereafter they moved to Fleurbaix from whence I think the first letters were written.

Early in July 1915 the West Riding Brigade moved to Ypres. It is hard to realise that the young man who penned the majority of these letters, was only 20 years old.

*This rough sketch map of the Western Front will help readers to
locate the various place names mentioned by my father.*

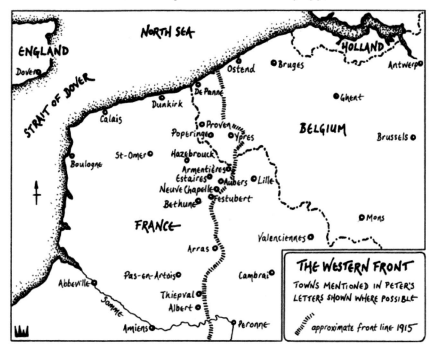

In order to help readers understand the conditions into which Peter and his young comrades found themselves pitched in 1915, I will try and illustrate with a few photographs

One of the first signs that the front line is getting nearer, vital supplies being brought to the front by mule train.

Mule Train

*Typical trench scene. Mud-caked, cold and wet, British soldier
eating his dinner of bully-beef outside his dug-out.*

*German shell-hole "somewhere in Flanders".
A deep fresh shell hole. Probably similar to the crater and destruction
where Walter Malthouse was killed beside Peter in May 1915.*

To the left a shell-hole large enough to drown a horse, in centre a great tree sectioned by a projectile; on the right a heap of earth sack defences.

Michael and his father, Peter visiting a War Grave Cemetery in Flanders in 1987, when Peter was 93..

Episode One

To France

The 5th Battalion, West Yorks Regt, join the B.E.F (British Expeditionary Force)

This is a copy of the clearest sample of a page of one of Peter's letters. Written in pencil on cheap paper.

One week after their arrival, on April 23rd 1915, Peter, now a Corporal, writes thus:

"The Battalion moved on to Estaires and that evening we marched into the forward area and into the trenches where we had a hot reception from the enemy rifle fire. It was most exciting to find onself in action for the first time and I fired several rounds at

the Hun trenches only 200 yards away. But I soon learned that random sniping at the enemy was fraught with danger, as the German snipers were deadly with their telescopic sights. We were in the front line trenches between Laventie and Neuve Chapelle and one of my Corporal friends was shot by a sniper in the chest – our first casualty.

One night I was detailed for a patrol between the lines and took six of my section with me – this was a hair-raising experience and we manned a listening post only 120 yards from the German trenches. All the time both sides fired star shells which illuminated the region of No-Man's Land and often fell near patrols or wiring parties. The barbed wire defences which helped to protect both front lines revealed the tragic picture of the recent battle of Neuve Chapelle, and were piled with the British dead which were entangled in the barbed wire; some could be seen wearing kilts. Even in our own small listening post there was the body of a dead member of the Essex Regiment. It was tragic that these gallant heroes could not be collected and buried. On these nocturnal patrols one could hear the constant screaming of rats which continued through the night – a most unpleasant reminder of the grim reality of war. After ten days in the front line my company was relieved and I had my first wash. We were told that we would be returning to the front line in readiness for a big attack – "Aubers Ridge".

On Sunday May 9th the whole Battalion went into action and a terrific bombardment of the German trenches at zero hour, 5 a.m., raged. Very soon the German counter-barrage was intense and no progress could be made. I had about ten of my section in my portion of the front line trench and we were taking what little cover we could from enemy shelling. Suddenly there was a terrific explosion and we all seemed to be blown up and the whole region was charged with the rank smell of explosive gases. I was partly buried by timber and trench debris and there seemed to be blood everywhere. One of my comrades, Walter Malthouse, (who was very close to me) was blown to pieces as he had received a direct hit from the heavy shell (high explosive) and was killed instantly. I was greatly stunned and shocked but felt that I had not been wounded, although I was only a few inches from my comrade. I found that two other friends had been wounded. This was a grim baptism to the reality of war and when I had been extricated from the gory shambles, I gathered up the shattered limbs and torso of my comrade (I knew his mother in Knaresborough, Yorkshire) and put them in a sand bag ready for burial. No stretcher bearers were available for this disaster, so we cleared up the shattered trench and dealt with the wounded. As the news of the tragedy spread along the front line we were visited by our Platoon Commander who was stunned to hear the details, and he told me that our Company Commander had been wounded in the neck and been carried on a stretcher to the Forward Dressing Station."

Note:

In 1988 when visiting Flanders with Lyn Macdonald and her veterans, "Doc" (as he was known) was brought face to face with Walter Malthouse's grave in Fauquissart Military Cemetery: seventy-three years after young Corporal Wilson had buried his friend! How proud he was to be asked to recite the immortal words:

Age shall not weary them
Nor the years condemn.
At the going down of the sun
And in the morning
We will remember them.

One of Lyn Macdonald's special surprises:
Peter, brought face to face with Walter Malthouse's grave in Fauquissart Cemetery,
supported by Lyn Macdonald and Colin Butler, gives an interview for the TV news.

After the Battle of Aubers Ridge the Battalion moved to Fleurbaix near the Belgian border, where the first two letters were written. Naturally, censorship of mail made it impossible for him to mention place names, or to go into much detail of their battles. His descriptions of some of their adventures in the trenches must have been desperately worrying for his parents and family!

First Letter

British Expeditionary Force, France
Sunday Afternoon June 13th 1915
1 John iii XIII Verse
"Marvel not my Brethren if the world hate you."

My dearest parents, Aunt and all,

Behold it is a glorious Sabbath Day and I have just returned from a swill at the Brewery about 3 miles from the firing line. This is my first decent wash for a fortnight, so you can well imagine how I enjoyed it. To my delight I had a clean shirt given unto me in exchange for my dirty tattered one and now I feel really clean and refreshed and shall I expect be free from the merciless attacks of the Jaspers[1]. Besides, I have just got a new pair of trousers and I can safely say that I have not got one of the aforesaid gentlemen on me – as they left me when I left the Brewery about an hour ago.

We have just arrived from rather an exciting period in the Trenches, and now I am billeted in a loft about an hour's march from the firing line. When in the trenches I was absolutely alive with them and notwithstanding a severe hunt every day – I could not dispense with my loving companions. The reason being that the straw in the trenches was absolutely alive with Jaspers. But I know as soon as I lie on the straw tonight I shall have one or two on by morning, but I have got quite used to them now and I don't worry in the least about them.

I must first thank Barbie and Mary for their most loving and welcome letters which afforded me much joy. I was so delighted to receive them as they were so full of interest. I also received Eddie's letter and yours together with his swell photo and the Yorks Herald. I think he looks simply fine in his OTC uniform. Now I offer you all my best wishes for the lovely parcel which arrived last night in perfect order. The bread was so fresh and the Cucumber as fresh as if just cut and I hope to enjoy it further for tea tonight. The waistcoat fits perfect and will do A1. I can assure you it will be most useful to me. I have just received a box of Chocolates from Selfridges as per W. C. Wilson Esq's kindness. Tell the girls that I enjoyed the Peppermints immensely and Barbie's cakes are most tasty.

I am glad you all had such a jolly day at Kirkham. I see that Barbara was not included in the party. No doubt this talented sweet pet fulfilled the duties of Mistress of the House during your absence. Barbie darling I think your drawings perfect and I can easily depict the new good work which you have most ably carried out in the garden. I am delighted that Madi is better and I hope she will enjoy her stay at Ashtree. I enclose

---

1 *Jaspers – the Tommies' name for lice which infested everyone's clothes and bedding.*

some photos which I hope you will keep for me. How do you like me in the blanket? This is from the Knaresborough Post and taken at Sutton. Mrs Walkinton very kindly sent me a parcel from Sutton and I enjoyed the contents immensely. I am so pleased you enjoyed the souvenirs and I hope they will interest you.

We have had a rather hard time this time in the trenches and have had very little sleep. And to our surprise during the last two days the Germans bombarded our trenches and several shells fell all around us. One hit the very dugout I was residing in and shook the abode like a wind does a tree. I wondered what was up and was very soon out into the trench, which was up to the boot tops in mud, and ready for what might come. Well, Whizz-Bang-Etc. came and very soon shrapnel was bursting and falling all over like Old Harry. A shell burst at one place then we all rushed in the opposite direction, and before we had gone 20 yards one burst about 10 yards away in a rotten ditch and covered several of us with mud and filth, which possessed an odour that one seldom enjoys. We quickly retraced our steps but the shells seemed to follow us and I thought it best to take cover behind the parapet and trust to luck – which we did with success, for in less than 5 minutes the boom of our heavy guns sent volleys of shells with deadly accuracy right into the German batteries and soon one could walk about in ease with only rifle fire to molest us.

The first 4 days reminded me of Africa and the last two of a swimming bath as a heavy thunder storm swept over us accompanied by the German Bombardment and really the noise was quite unique. The bursting of shells and then thunder crashes together with the light of the explosions was a sight one seldom sees. I was asleep in what I thought sunshine and suddenly a deluge swept over us and being dog tired I did not wake up until I was laid in about 2 or 3 inches of water! After an attempt to drain my dugout for about 10 minutes, the thunderstorm started again and I went outside and the trench was swimming and I had only gone about 10 strides when I performed the "Gaby Glide" and was instantly laid on my back full length in mud and water, but being wet through the latter, although unpleasant, was only a mere detail.

I have just finished tea, having greatly enjoyed the Figs, Cucumber, Bread and Barbie's delicious cakes which Kirby and I think most lovely. Hence I will proceed with my Epistle which I hope will cheer you one and all. I will proceed when pay is over as I must be present to look after a few necessaries. Exit.

Pay over and I have just got a 10 franc sub and now I can send you another parcel of souvenirs, as money is very scarce here. I hope to send you a parcel about Wed'day and you should receive the consignment about Sunday and as soon as you receive it let me know – then I will be at rest. I will also send under separate cover tomorrow about half a doz. post cards which I got under thrilling circumstances between the two firing lines. You will find them interesting and good souvenirs. I got them myself.

Now about that letter which was found in a case on the battlefield. I can't say whether the soldier was killed – no address is stated and I don't think you could find the address.

Of course if you can send the letter to the intended person do so, but understand I can't give security that the writer was killed.

The next parcel will contain a German Shell case, Shrapnel not exploded, a splendid uncommon souvenir. The interior exploded but the case luckily did not. A German Copper Shell Head – (splendid specimen) also German Aluminium Shell Head (good specimen). A few pieces of Shrapnel and a German Helmet which unluckily has been robbed of its chief beauties but the helmet formation is there and notwithstanding the absence of the latter I think it is quite a good souvenir. If the weight is too much I will forward the surplus weight next parcel. Also a few German bullets which have come near to me.

The Germans are playing "Old Harry" and are bombarding some buildings near here with their big guns. Unluckily they have killed 3 and wounded several, and have caused a rumpus with the horses – killing a few. My legs have been rather bad during the past few days and I think it is Rheumatism caused by so much wet. I have not had much rest lately while in the trenches. However a few pills and a good rest have put me on the move and I am the same "Jolly Pierre". You would notice that our Casualties were the largest in that Herald received yesterday. 4 being in my Co. Cook thanks you for the cigars and he is at present cleaning up the dixies which contained our tea. It was a peculiar sight to see our fellows cleaning out dirty ditches this morning, whilst over the fields one could hear the Church-bells.

To my delight I was richly blessed this morning and thanks be to my dear Lord,I was able to wend my way to his Altar and partake of the of the Holy Eucharist. This time I went to the same temporary church in the old Brewery but thank God I was able to take with me no less than a dozen from my Company. The service was too beautiful and all of us went to pour out our various thanksgivings with great joy. We had to take our Rifles, Bandoliers and Respirators with us and how strange it looked to gaze at a pile of rifles (our best earthly friend in this war here), which rested against the wall. I thought, as I knelt at the sweet morning hour, of you all at home and well knew that you also were partaking of the same great service and my prayers, I feel sure, ascended with yours unto the throne of Grace. Fancy being at the same great service at the same time as you, but the spell of distance between us is great. Nevertheless I tried to imagine that you were all present with me. God grant that very soon I may be with you in our dear church at home.

I am really so happy here notwithstanding the circumstances. What joy and comfort I receive from my dear Lord when I am in prayer and meditation with him. Although my prayers are frequently hasty, I know greatly to my joy and comfort that my blessed Saviour offers them to the throne for me. This war, thank God has brought many soldiers to their knees in repentance and I have, through his mercies, been able to afford them some earthly comforts and I rejoice to do what little I can in honour of his sacred name. How much they appreciate home now – really I have seen this war to be the means of many blessings in disguise.

Hullo the mail has come. Cook has gone to see if there are any letters for me which is most likely. I have thanked my God that he has given me courage to speak boldly to some of his fallen flock here and I rejoice to see that some are seeking his guidance in various ways. I pray earnestly that I may well receive the Gift of the Holy Spirit, that I may be blessed with bringing even the deepest sinner to the realm of true happiness in my dear Lord. Oh pray for me that strength and courage, through his spirit, will be allotted unto me, as many golden chances are presenting themselves. No greater joy will be mine than to bring a fallen one back to the fold, where true joy and happiness reign unceasingly for those who trust and ask of the many many blessings he graciously bestows upon all.

Now I want you to send me that Cig. Case which was in that box from Sutton – but my dearest ones don't think for a moment that the Smoke charm is coming upon me. Reg gave it to me and it will be useful as we get wet often here and I only smoke very seldom to prevent any fever from these terrible smells which are numerous here. So comfort yourselves regarding this habit. I fell in a French cess arrangement the other day, it was covered up with straw and I had to discard my trousers as they were too savoury to accompany me! I rejoice to hear about the Garden and all my favourite possessions and the Cucumber was lovely - and so fresh. Thanks so much for the sweet knife and the pencils which will suit A1.

Well my dearest ones all. I pray that I shall soon be able to behold your dear faces and God Grant that in his mercies he will guide me safely through these many great dangers and bring me safely home again in peace. I am glad that dearest Mother and Aunt keep well. All this is so comforting to me. Don't worry about me. Forgive me for not writing often when in the trenches as I have no time and get so tired. Well good-bye dearest ones and give my best wishes to all friends. With united love and with the abiding presence of our dear Lord I commit my body and soul unto his divine care – God grant that very soon I may be returned to you in peace and love, and that the rich blessing of our divine Lord will rest upon you all is the unceasing prayer of.

Ever your most loving Son and Brother.

A G WILSON   1416

P.S. Fondest love. Kisses to all xxxxxxxx

Second Letter

British Expeditionary Force
France
Sunday 27th June 1915

"I reckon that the sufferings of this present time are not worthy to be compared with the Glory which shall be revealed in us". Rom. Viii. 18v

My dearest parents and <u>all</u>,

O nce again I find myself in communication with Home, Sweet Home, on this glorious Sabbath morn. This time I am laid on my oilsheet in a French Cherry Orchard near the firing line, with about 2 lbs of lovely cherries (and so sweet too) so you see I am going to enjoy myself. Why shouldn't I? I much regret that I cannot go to the Holy Communion or even a Church service. The nearest church, and a glorious one it was too, is a heap of ruins and to gaze upon this sacred abode of the Almighty is too pitiful to describe. Surely the Almighty will avenge this terrible work of the Hun and very soon bestow upon the Allies the blessings of an early and sure victory. We have had very heavy rains here and the crops have almost burst into a new resurrection. Even bird life is joyful at the presence of pearly rain notwithstanding the awful din of cannon and the fierce raging battle where our gallant sons are fighting for victory at a very dear price.

The rest of this letter is missing. Peter's memoirs give a graphic account of dawn in the trenches which will help to set the scene:

When in the trenches at Fleurbaix, each morning at 'stand-to' (at dawn) all the troops had to use a special gauze respirator covering the nose and mouth – this precaution had to be taken owing to the Germans using heavy tear gas, which they released if the wind was favourable – blowing the gas towards our trenches. Before being placed over the mouth and nose the gauze respirator was soaked in urine, which had been contained in large tins which were used by the troops during the night. Much to the relief of the troops this vital period of "stand-to" only lasted for about 10-15 minutes.

Early in July 1915 the West Riding Brigade moved into Belgium, to the YPRES sector.

During the long march into Belgium we had no billets and slept in barns and sheds when we could and on one occasion I slept in a hen house with legs over the perch. I had a good night's sleep and in the early morning was amazed to see a large grand cockerel turn his head sideways to view his visitor. About 30 hens did not worry about my being there.

Third Letter

British Expeditionary Force
Belgium
5th Sunday after Trinity – 4.7.15

"But and if ye suffer for righteousness sake, happy are ye:
And be not afraid of their terror, neither be troubled, But sanctify the Lord God in your hearts".
I St Pet iii

My dearest Parents and All,

I have been longing to begin this family epistle and after about 6 hours of varied interruptions I hereby commence. I have left my noisy comrades near the billet and to obtain quietness I have retired to a shady corner of the large field which adjoins the billet, my only trouble now being the intense heat and the Belgian flies. The heat is terrible and England never has such a temperature – besides we get so little wind here which, if present, always tempers the heat. We have done some long marches this week and as you will see we have moved up country and have crossed over the border into the territory of our gallant little Ally, whose inhabitants are much kinder and more hospitable in every way than the French people who, without a doubt, rob us right and left.

The other night we marched a long way in torrential heat and rain and for over 6 hours trouped along wet through and perspiring all the time, as if under Turkish Bath treatment. I never had such a march throughout all our training. With over 50 lbs of kit pulling down your shoulders – your shirt wet through with sweat, together with furious attacks of Belgian Jaspers *(lice)* who without a doubt are even more vicious than their Allied neighbours, made the whole business nearly unbearable. The heat was in many cases too much for the fellows and with the huge weight, as well being wet through, one could see many a worn out comrade being compelled to drop out for a rest.

I had a most exciting time having 3 cruel nails furiously ploughing their way into my feet, which so far have been wonderful. The roads are all stony and rough. However, tired and with hearts still glowing, we arrived at this pretty little place where, for the past week we have been enjoying a well earned rest. Last night we had a route march and for almost 2 hours we trudged along in a dust like a November fog – the reason being we were passing countless horses and guns moving after dark so as to avoid being seen by hostile Aircraft. It was really surprising to look across country and see the dust far away rising from the wending roads as we went along – and at times I could not see the men a few yards in front of me – it was really almost like crossing a desert – How the cucumber from home sustained my parched throat after the intense heat and parades. I was soon asleep under a tree in this field and slept like a top all night. By the way I have been sleeping out all the last week and the other night a cow put its foot upon me and caused rather an unusual awakening! I have had a nice quiet day today and have been bare-footed almost all day. I have had my shirt off all morning – so you see I will not be bothered by the heat when it is possible to evade it.

I now offer you all thanks for your letters which needless to say I am always delighted to receive. The latest one to arrive is Mary's which has just been handed to me, written Thursday last. I was delighted to receive Barbie's long, beautiful and welcome epistle and rejoice to read that all in the garden is looking so well. By the way how are the huge oriental thistles Mrs. Plant gave to me? – I hope they are a success as these plants are a picture when at maturity. Many thanks for the welcome parcel which charmed me, and all therein arrived in splendid condition. The ham was lovely, I can't express the delicious taste it afforded me. Barbie's cakes were simply lovely and I greatly enjoyed them. By all means still send Bread and Butter. I so enjoy this home food and the butter always arrives in such good order. I am delighted, Mother darling, with the writing case which will be most useful to me. The tablets will be reserved for the trenches – which place I think we are bound for in a few days – no doubt we shall have lively times as we are going into the thick of it now – although I think we have been there long enough already. The flies here seem to be a great pest to the cows, who keep galloping past me with their "Rudders" in the air like a pack of hounds – it is really a funny sight.

I received a nice letter from the Bank with the usual good news for the end of the Quarter. Fancy, I have been up nearly a year and I think it looks like being another yet. It is really hard to realise all the glories of the Sabbath here. I can see in front of me now, 1st the Belgians working among the Stock etc, and, far away, under clumps of trees small groups of soldiers gambling away as hard as they can. It is impossible to stop this act as the fellows are so tired and have nothing else to do – also they have no place to spend their money. On the dusty roads the transports are busy doing their valuable work. Above the watchful Aeroplanes are doing their patrols. Thus you will see what a Sabbath is like in this part of Europe.

Rather a funny coincidence happened on Friday, I was eagerly reading your account of Capt. Sowerby's visit, when only a few yards away the gallant Capt. was just returning to billets from his leave – this was quite funny n'est pas! I hope he has had a good time and I call him jolly lucky – I say, the sun is terribly hot now and my neck, face and arms are as brown as a chestnut and I look quite a navvy, with my hair cut as short as it possibly can be. You would go almost dotty if you saw me! It is quite striking to see the large numbers of very old Belgians which are about here, and it is plain to see where all the gallant sons of our brave little Ally are – Namely fighting for their very existence against her terrible, cruel and inhuman foe. The girls here make some lovely lace and I should love to send you some. I have just finished my washing – my shirt, socks, towel etc. are now patiently awaiting the kindness of the Sun. The socks will do very well and thick ones are best. I should like some tooth paste, tooth brush and a

Razor please, and don't forget to send the cig. Case next parcel. Cook thanks you very much for the cigars and he hopes you are well.

I say – the Whistle has blown, some hostile aircraft in sight and far away I can see one of the German dirigibles or zeppelins – it is a monster but the wretch takes good care to keep well over its own lines – out of our gun range and out of our aeroplanes' reach. I have got so used to seeing German forms of aircraft that if one comes over I just gaze at it as if it, were one of our own. The rest has been quite a relief in many ways. The nerves are resting and the intense and awful odours are absent and no great guns booming out right behind you – and last but not least, a good wash and a really good sleep. I hope to send you several P.C.s showing some of the awful work of the wicked Hun in a few days and I should like the Vicar to see them – By the way has he seen my souvenirs yet? I hope he will be interested in them.

Thank God again for his great blessings to me. This morning I attended a Celebration of the Holy Communion and the blessed service was the most real and impressive one I think I have ever attended. Only about a dozen attended, yet the service was so real and meant so much to me. The service was held behind a large flax stack in the open. A small table with a white cloth thereon and candles and a small cross was the picture that presented itself to all partakers of the Body and Blood of our Blest Redeemer at this solemn service. Even the birds and nature seemed to know that their Creator was somewhere in their midst and with the early morning sun blazing down through the cloudless realms of sky upon the few bareheaded servants of the Divine Lord – it was under the above circumstances such as I shall never forget, that I had intimate communion with my God. I felt many times that even you dear ones at home were joining in supplication with me and although far away in body – yet something told me that our praises and prayers ascended together towards the mercy seat of God – where, when this mortal life is o'er and we are called to our eternal peace, we may as a family fall down before our blest Redeemer and for ever, with those countless celestial choirs, praise and worship our King and Lord.

The old prophecy came before me. How, that in times of old, the faithful wended their way to the Dens and Caves and remote parts of the earth to hold this solemn service with their divine Lord – Little did I think that such a thing was possible during these present times. I hope to attend a C. of E. Service tonight in the open somewhere here. One thing quite struck me here, when the boys leave church and as soon as they get outside, they at once begin to play pitch and toss with coins and other forms of gambling – it was quite a startler for many of our Tommies.

Now I am going to surprise you a little – Tomorrow's post should favour you with a letter from Beckett's Bank, Knaresboro'. The letter will contain two cheques, one £3/3/- which is to go towards a holiday for the members of the family – Now don't think me foolish – I want you dear ones to have a holiday – It will do you good – if you don't go to the seaside, go to some relatives or Knaresboro as Mrs Stimson[2] can

---

2 *Mrs Stimson must have been his landlady when he was working for the bank.*

put you up and have a jolly good time – Try and think there is not such a thing as this cruel war. I have several pounds due from the Army besides my bank screw, which I am lucky to get, as I think I am about the only one in my Co. getting full pay during the war. Nothing will please me more than to see you, my dearest ones, at home having a holiday – make the best of the time – So don't for a moment think me rash – it is the intense wish of your soldier son at the front who, though I have to rough it a bit, thinks that you should (as many of you as possible) have a holiday. So my dearest ones think out your place and go, for it doesn't signify that if I have a bit of roughing, you should go short. Think of the time, when, if my blessed Lord answers my earnest prayers, that he in His mercy will bring me home again in peace – what Joy there will be! God grant that the day is nigh at hand.

The second cheque will be for £2/2/-. This is for the Sunday School in my own dear parish. A thank offering to Almighty God for his countless blessings to me during the past. I should like you to get good serviceable Hymn Books for the Scholars, as I think for that amount you can get a sufficient supply suitable for the members of the Scholars who can read. If you prefer Bibles then get them – and above all if you desire any more cash I shall be delighted to remit another cheque – so don't hold for a moment, Pater darling. I want to do this little part for our Sunday School ….
(Note: Remainder of letter missing.)

EARLY JULY

We soon took over an advanced position of the trench system North of Ypres at Turco Farm, as our portion of the front line was known, about the most advanced station on the British Front. Here I was able to spot huge mortar shells as they tore through the air from the German mortar positions. I got quite expert in spotting these huge shells and soon learned that one must fix one's gaze well in front of the roar of the rapidly moving shell. At night the ration parties, brought up by gallant drivers with their mule teams, had an assembly point not far from the famous Bridge 4 on the Yser Canal. Of course the German Gunners were well aware that the assembled limbers, with mules and mounted drivers, made highly visible targets with all the rations and fresh water for the troops manning the trenches in the Ypres Salient.

Frequently the fierce bombardment caused heavy casualties to the gallant drivers, their mules and the collection ration parties.

The sight which greeted the troops on their way to the front: Ypres in ruins.

A sketch by Peter of Bridge 4 on the Yser Canal

A photograph of the same bridge from the archives of the P.O.W. Own Regiment of Yorkshire Museum archives. Note all the dugouts on the far bank – like water rat holes!

Fourth Letter

I feel so sorry for Mrs D and Mr Jack, I fear the penalty will come sooner than later. I am rather bored today; not annoyed, the reason being that I am on fatigue all day and have no time to devote to this family epistle as I would like. Being Sunday makes the business rather worse – fancy brick layering all day and navvying – I am laying a path through the sloppy undergrowth by means of broken bricks etc. But Sunday is nothing in War time so we will fight on. About 2 months ago I spent a Sunday cleaning out dirty ditches – However it's got to be done.

I actually had a swim in this famous canal 3 days ago, which is within rifle shot of the Germans. I could not get a bath and felt so muzzy that I went in and I felt much better after my exciting dip. After about half an hour the Huns sent about half a dozen shells, right in and about the place where only a few minutes before I had been swimming. The shells caused the water to rise over 100 feet into the air and after about 5 minutes the surface of the water was covered by the forms of some large dead fish and countless smaller ones. Several tommies hastily procured some of the larger fish and I had the pleasure of eating some, for supper, slain by German shells.

We have had very heavy rain lately and the place gets filthy, the soil being so clay-like.

Yes! I enjoyed the fruit immensely and the apples were lovely – my thoughts flew to that tree on the rose path where once the apples grew. I have just had a refreshing drink of Lemonade made from the crystals. It is delicious. Oh, thank Mr Ward for the Lobster which was lovely. I enjoyed it immensely. I hope Eddie dear you are well after all your exciting holidays.

How do you like your temporary situation now, Barbie darling? The people are very nice and as you say a respected family in the ancient city. Your first page is sweet and I treasure those comforting words very deeply. Now Mary old girl how are you going along – No doubt you get plenty of exciting times. How is your War post? I hope you get a job as everybody will admire you – You are the people that will help to win the war.

I don't think that there will be any of this town left with its once glorious Cathedral in ruins. The Germans send Jack Johnsons over every day and they sound like express trains as they pass overhead on their terrible errands. Please excuse this awful hand – I have no rest and no firm back to write upon. I hope that you dear ones are all well and I trust that the visit to Knaresboro will do all who go good.

I saw Capt. Sowerby yesterday and he looks very well – his new post will be much nicer for him. We have had some swimming sports today in this canal – fancy sports within 2000 yards of the German lines. During the whole time the guns were very busy and their reports came down the valley like thunder. The powder from Boots has caused terrible havoc among the Jaspers and now I have got the numbers well under subjection. Oh I would <u>specially</u> like to know what sort of fruit are the young currants turning out – the ones you set upon the wood wall on the rose path, in the place of the old collection. Are the nuts a success? I hope you have got some nice books for the Sunday School – how many have you purchased? I am so pleased the shell noses are safe – they will be such a valuable souvenir, as all souvenirs of the war are forbidden now.

I fear poor Mrs Hunt is very ill and I expect she will have a long and slow recovery – she has been ill ever since I left York.

Well my dearest ones, I will say goodbye as I have no more news for you. I sincerely trust you are all well and happy. I will close by committing you all unto the safe keeping and protection of our divine Lord. I pray that he may shower down upon you all his richest blessings and that very soon he will bless us with a righteous and lasting peace. My fondest love and kisses to you all. MIZPAH.*

Believe me,
Ever your loving Son etc.
A G WILSON   XXXXXX

Peace, perfect Peace
In this dark world of Sin,
The blood of Jesus whispers,
Peace within.

*MIZPAH – I think this word is an association with Peter's strong Sunday School upbringing in HAXBY. There were several Old Testament happenings in places called MIZPAH, e.g. where Jacob and Laban made a covenant (Gen. 31.49)
MIZPAH is also regarded as an emotional bond between people who are separated (either physically or by death). The word "mizpah" can often be found on headstones in cemeteries and on other memorials. "And Mizpah; for he said, The Lord watch between me and thee, when we are absent one from another." This is clearly the meaning my father intends when he closes his letters with MIZPAH.

Fifth Letter

British Expeditionary Forces
Belgium
7th Sunday after Trinity
18 7 15

I will say unto the Lord Thou art my hope and my strong hold:
My God, in him will I trust. Psm xci v 2

My dearest Parents and All,

As I am still within rifle fire and in reserve dugouts I fear I shall only be able to let you have a short epistle. Also I shall still be in the firing line next Sunday and goodness only knows when we shall return to billets, and once again see the Belgians. I have just sent off a PC to let you know that I am better and also to acknowledge the various kind letters and the glorious parcel which charmed me. Many thanks for the delicious assortment which, needless to say, provided me with many enjoyable snacks. Cook was delighted with the cigars and also thanks for soap and cigs etc.

The rain here is most troublesome and has caused me endless bother this week. My dugout having been swilled out both at night and day and every night my hard bed has been saturated. I feel several pains in my shoulders and back, which I am pleased to say are gradually going. I have not washed my shirt for about a month and I shall delight in having a wash when we return to the baths where they will give us a clean shirt. In these trenches you can't get a wash – my only wash is in a mug and I swill my face with my shaving brush – this performance, although the best under the circumstances, is much appreciated I can tell you.

We are busy working night and day and carry heavy loads to the trenches during the darkness and generally it pours in torrents all the time – you return to your swimming dugout, yourself wet through, and sleep for a time and find yourself probably a little drier by sunrise. This has been the "carry-on" almost all this week and today for a change the sun is shining at intervals. The Huns have been shelling us almost all the week and on Friday they put some gas shells right amongst us. The pain caused to my eyes was terrible. The cruel stuff is not what I should like to contend with again. However now I feel quite fit and as happy as the lambs in Spring. So none of you need worry that I am ill, because now I am quite well and the same frolicsome "Pierre".

One Corporal, a great friend of mine, and others have been killed this spell. The Cpl. was a fine young fellow with a brilliant prospect in front of him. We spent many pleasant hours together whilst we garrisoned Sutton-on-Sea. I am so sorry for him poor fellow. He was shot in the head and died without pain. I have written a letter to one of his intimate friends and I hope this sad case in many, will be borne with Divine help and comfort by his parents and friends.

I am glad you like the souvenirs and p.cards – what do you think of the beautiful wire cutters? They came from a dead officer who lay between the firing lines. You need not fear about me crawling after German helmets any more, as an order came out yesterday that no more war souvenirs would be allowed to go home – besides I value my head above all souvenirs[3] – I had packed two lovely French bayonets and sent them off but on account of the restriction they were returned, much to my disappointment – they were lovely specimens and would have caused no end of interest. I am in a very uncomfortable position being laid flat on my stomach in my dugout with my equipment as rest - so forgive any mistakes and the bad hand. I am pleased you have kept the shell heads – they are good specimens.

I am writing to Mr Watson and am asking him to invest £50 in the War Loan for me. I think Mr Smith's letter is so cheering and as usual full of good humour – I feel sure Australia will put him on the road to good health. My back aches so I must take a rest or lie in some other position. However the latter is a mere detail so I will proceed.

I am delighted to read the good news about the lovely garden. My joy is great to read that the thistles are such a success – now mind that Barbie looks after saving some seeds or cuttings. I well knew that you would be pleased with them as they quite took me by storm when I saw them at Mrs Plants. Oh, how did Mr Watson and family enjoy their visit to Haxby? No doubt the Boss would be delighted with the Garden etc. I hope you will get Robinson over for the weekend. He would so enjoy it and he is sending me a razor over this week.

I am delighted to hear that you are going to Knaresboro for your holidays. Mrs Stimson will put you up – you know that the old lady is dead, so she can put plenty of attention upon you both. Now write soon and book the room as all the public are flocking to inland health resorts on account of the fear of hostile aircraft. I hope the girls will have a jolly good day there and tell Mary a punt is as safe as a house, and by all means have a little cruise upon the mossy waters of the picturesque Nidd. Let me know when you are going and I hope good weather will favour you. Tell Barbie her cakes were most tasty and I enjoyed them immensely, also I was charmed to receive her long lovely epistle which I have read several times. Mary darling I was delighted to receive your lengthy epistle and I hope you were successful in obtaining your post- Don't forget to let me know the result. Yes, old girl, take out a punt and have a good time. Tell Madi dear that I am so pleased she is well and feels so much better and I hope she will like my little business home at K. Are you taking Flop with you or will she be at School also? I should like dearest Aunt Pol to partake in some of the joy. How is dear Old Aunt, I suppose her help in the garden is most valuable n'est pas? So sorry to hear about poor old Willie Sharp. I do hope his wound will not be serious.

---

3 *I had begun to wonder!*

Now dearest ones a word about the other £2-2-0. I did not know about the prosperous position of the Sunday School. It is my sincere wish that the gift should be given to the Lord, as I wish to offer the latter small gift to the honour and glory of his holy name. I would like you to give £1-1-0 to Barbie for her K.M. work, and the other for my missionary box or any other charity which you think needs funds. So dearest Pater I think I have made this little item plain and hope you approve of it.

Hullo this valley, with its canal, is fairly rolling with the peal and roar of mighty guns even on this Sabbath day. This is a cruel Sunday, everybody working and me orderly Sergt. and I cannot even retire behind a tree in order to read through the services of the Holy Communion, Litany and Psalms. I hope to snatch a few seconds tonight so that I can hold intimate communion with my guide and blessed companion. I am in demand all day and it is wonderful how I have written you so much – but I fear it will be uninteresting as I have had so many breaks. Oh I am going to have some Cucumber for tea. I did so enjoy all the other good things – they all arrived as if just having been carried from storeroom to the dining room. There are some huge shells whizzing over now and the noise is like countless thunderstorms. I delight to read that the tennis court looks so well and I should have loved to have witnessed the thrilling duel between Pater and Co. I hope you received my last Sunday Epistle which was written within a mile of here. Mrs Lofthouse very kindly sent Cpl. B a parcel and I have reciprocated.

Well dearest ones, I must close, I have to parade men for tea and I want to get this letter off – so please excuse the abrupt ending. So dearest ones, I will say good-bye and don't be alarmed, I am as fit as ever. I sincerely hope you are all well and that Mother dear is quite in the best of health. I was so pleased to receive her letters with dear Dad's this morning. They so cheered me up I can joyfully say.

Well "au revoir" my dearest ones and the Lord bless you and keep you all, the Lord lift up the light of his Countenance upon you all and grant you all his richest blessings of peace, and finally soon bring me safely back to you in joy and peace unbounded, is the prayer of your

Ever dear and loving son, etc.

Arthur G Wilson xxxxxxxx

"Oh refine me by Thy Spirit
Make my earthly life sublime,
With my heart a home for Jesus,
Till I'm done with earth and time."

P.S. Return map herewith you kindly sent me.

Sixth Letter

British Expeditionary Force
27 July 15

"The Lord is on my side: I will not fear what man doeth unto me."
Psalm CVIII verse vi

My dearest parents and all,

I was so sorry that I could not send you my usual Sunday epistle as we were moving and no letters were dispatched. However it is better late than never, so herewith I will let you have a few details which I hope will interest you all. I must first thank you sincerely for the exquisite parcel which arrived in tip top order on Saturday last. I enjoyed all the contents immensely and I think Pater is a perfect genius. His packing abilities appear to me as wonderful, as everything in the parcels arrives in a perfect condition.

Several comrades of no mean rank have passed many complimentary remarks towards the talented packer and addresser of "Lucky Peter's" parcels.

Well dearest ones you will be pleased to hear that once again I am out of the trenches and the long spell finished – alas 4 more of my favourite comrades have passed through the narrow gate in the last week. One poor fellow, my favourite in my Co., who has been uncommonly kind to me, was hit by a sniper in the neck and in my arms passed away to his perfect peace. Much to my relief he suffered very little; alas I could do nothing for him as he was mortally wounded and bled internally.

We have been in a terribly lively hole and we were in parts less than 100 yards from the German trenches. All the time the trenches were in a terrible state – nothing but mud, flies and water and the Germans shelled us night and day.

I fear we shall get very little rest as already we have made a name for ourselves. Kitchener has termed us as the finest Territorial Div. in France and has remarked to His Army that he hopes that they will prove themselves equal to our gallant Div. Two days ago I witnessed a marvellous and thrilling aerial duel in which the German was hurled to the earth with his machine in flames.

Now I must thank all the Girls, Edie, Mother dear, and Pater for their most cheery and welcome epistles, which needless to say charmed me. How nice Mr. Smith writing to you Mother dear. I am so pleased he is well and I am writing to him soon. I am quite surprised to read that Murville (*a cousin, Murville Hull, whose family emigrated to New Zealand*) is coming to France and trust that our loving Father will guide him and strengthen him in all his trials, which are so many in this terrible war and grant him health and a safe and quick return home to his dear ones.

You can get a most useful writing tablet from the penny Bazaar, which will be very handy on a job like this. Oh, by the way, will you please send me a strong shaving glass, in a kind of metal mounted case about 3" by 4" so that it will be strong and handy to carry. I have to shave every two days when we are in billets, so you see I need a glass.

I am so pleased that the garden is so prosperous. How I long for a roam in my glorious domain. I hope the 5 silk P. cards arrived safely yesterday and in a nice clean condition. I was delighted to read the several epistles of the girls and to read that they spent such a happy day – I sincerely trust that you dearest Mother, Aunt and Pater will spend a similar time when you go to Knaresboro. I feel sure you will find Mrs. Stimson uncommonly cheap and she will …
(*page missing*)
out a bit. It will do him a power of good. Please send him a 5/- P.Order from me and I will forward the same to you – I hope it will not be too late – as I think he is going for a fortnight. I expect Mr. Watson will be sending you a certificate for £50 War Loan for me, any day now. Mr. Robinson has sent me a lovely safety razor – a perfect Gem.

Now Pater dear, thin the grapes out cruelly – don't have any mercy – they will be better for it. Well all my dear ones I must close as the mail is almost due. I saw Capt. S. ce matin and he looks much better. Blow the flies! They are swarming around me in millions.

Well dearest ones good bye and I pray that the richest blessings of our blest Redeemer will be showered upon you all. Praying earnestly that He will soon grant this world an everlasting peace and with health, joy and strength, grant me a happy return home to my dearest ones is the unceasing supplication of
Ever your most loving Son etc.

Arthur G Wilson
Xxxxxxxxxxxxxxx

"Peace perfect Peace."

Seventh Letter

B. Ex. Force
8 August 1915
10th Sunday after Trinity ?
In-the-Trenches

"O Lord, let it be Thy pleasure to deliver me:
make haste, O Lord, to help me.
Thou art my helper and Redeemer; make no long
Tarrying, O my God. Psalm XL. Verses 16 x 21

My dearest Parents and all,

As it is too late in the day to get this epistle off I have just despatched a Foreign Service Post Card to acknowledge the glorious parcel with all its goodly contents received in the best of condition, even to the glorious potted meat and tomatoes. The latter appearing as if just fresh pulled and they were as firm as a rock and so tasty.

I regret to state that this letter will have to be very much shorter, as I have severely gashed the middle finger – a cruel deep gash from the 2nd joint right up to the middle of the root of the finger nail. The nail having stayed the cut and prevented the remaining part of the finger being severed from the bone. The cut, although deep and nasty, is nothing to chirrup about and is a mere detail compared with the terrible wounds which our brave tommies are receiving here. No doubt in a few days I shall be perfectly alright again. So you need not worry in the least as a cut is a wound which soon mends.

Of course I reported sick this morning and upon going down with the party some German snipers spotted us and sent several bullets right into our midst. However we were soon lain flat and we all escaped injury and only got mud and water up to the neck. The bullets came ping-ping between our legs and after shouting a little, I got all the party into a trench and we were soon on the way to the Dressing station, as I well knew the Germans would send some small shrapnel into us. Well we arrived at the Dressing Station, although several of the party were terribly bad and just behind us we heard the whiz of shells, which exploded just above the trench which had concealed us only 2 minutes before. One fellow of another Regiment got hit with shrapnel in the wrist and thigh. The Dr. of course looked to see if my wound (cut) was clean and was pleased to see that it was. He said it would heal quickly.

I thought I would go another way back and took one poor fellow with me who was terribly nervous. He was in a terrible state. We started and although we were well under cover in a good but wet trench, he shivered and crouched as if we were on the top of a front line trench. All went well until about 1/4 mile from our trenches, when all of a sudden, the Germans started to shell and put about 8 or 10 shells right on to the top of us, sending mud and earth high into the air and covering us with earth etc. Well the poor fellow was a terrible mess, shivering and perspiring terribly – I lay flat in the bottom of the trench with him and as soon as the shells stopped off he tore down the trench like a hare, with me after him and after an exciting rush we gained our trenches. I was very pleased indeed that I got him safely back without mishap and really this Sunday morning was most exciting and rather unpleasant.

You will no doubt read of the big Artillery Bombardments around this …… District. The roar of the big guns is terrible and they roar night and day and I feel sure they can be heard for miles. One huge shell fell into our trenches and made a hole deep enough and wide enough to conceal a house – a remarkable sight. Really I don't know what to think. I regret to say that the true Christian chum of mine – the one who went with me on that long tramp to the Holy Communion some 10 weeks ago, has got shot in the knee and is badly wounded and gone to the Casualty Clearing Station – from there he will go to England. When he writes to me I think he will probably be in Hospital in York or not far away. I should feel much relieved and pleased if you would see him some time if possible. He is a fine young fellow and I have told him several things about you at home and he would be delighted to see you. But worse than that; poor Cpl. Ted Baker of my Co., the great chum of Oswald and myself, was killed by a shell yesterday. He always enjoyed my parcels – as likewise I enjoyed his and he is about 25 and is in business in London. (Good Billet.) Now I will mention something most remarkable about what he said. Only the day after he was killed he would have left this Battalion and would have got his transfer to the Motor Corps., miles away behind the lines. He said, you know I have almost got my transfer and if I thought there was anything in the text (which I will mention later) I would not bother to go but stay with you. The text is this:
"*Whosoever seeketh to save his life shall lose it*".
And on Friday last a shell went right into his dugout and killed the poor fellow instantly. Fancy him saying the above startling words only a few days ago. I am so sorry for him and his dear people and his young lady, a nice girl whom he is engaged to, will be broken hearted. I must write to her. We have had many jolly times together, both in England and out here. Well it is the Almighty's will and he works in a very mysterious way and we must all bow in perfect submission to his divine will.

Fancy another Sunday in the trenches and we shall still be in next Sunday as well. However we must wait and trust wholly in the Divine Lord who will order all things. My thoughts suddenly flew to the Altar rails of my dear little parish church at home this morning at 8 to 8.30 and something seemed to link me spiritually with you dear ones who were there to offer up your petition to the throne of Grace. My prayers also arose from my heart in true faith and I pray that they ascended linked with yours to the Mercy Seat of our Divine Creator and Redeemer. You cannot realize what it feels like, fancy I have not had a normal Sunday since March last. I trust that the Almighty will bring this terrible war to a close 'ere many moons wax and wane.

Now dearest ones I hope you received my additional epistle last Sunday and that it found you all well and in good spirits. Now a word about the delicious parcel. I had just a quarter of a loaf of bread and a tin of Bully for the day's rations and all of a sudden your godsend arrived at my dugout – You dear ones could not possibly realise my deep joy which arose upon the receipt of the splendid gift! The tomatoes were lovely – the potted meat so fresh and so tasty– the mirror will do Top Hole, a splendid thing – thanks for other sundries.

I think this letter is much, much longer than I expected to scribe and my chum will think I am going to finish his pad. Oh the Thirstlets are lovely and in the desired condition – many thanks. I am always so delighted to receive any messages from my dear home. I received the Times for which I thank you and enjoyed reading it. I am glad you have such a good crop of fruit and that the garden is so flourishing. Any more visitors for the souvenirs? I don't much approve of your situation Barbie from your account – they more or less have you for a mug or run-about – although the family is a good one. I enjoyed your description, it is most interesting. Now Mary old girl, how are you getting on – I suppose you will miss Madi and Florence. Have you done any War Work yet?

Oh – Now don't think me greedy but I think the maximum price for parcels is 1/7d, and some parcels which come here are in large biscuit tins and tin boxes, so don't be afraid of weight. But I am more than satisfied and those large biscuit tins are expensive. Really Dad you are a marvel at packing and I get crowds round me to watch me unpack the box of Dainties.

Well dearest ones, goodbye – I really must close and I am really very well and fit and I hope you dear ones at home are all well. My best wishes to all inquiring friends. I will finish the letter by committing you all unto the Divine Lord, that He in his mercy will bless you all with his rich blessings.

My fondest love and kisses to you all.
Good Bye au present and MIZPAH.
Believe me.

Ever your most loving Son.
Arthur G Wilson, Cpl.
Xxxxxxxxxxxxxxxxx

Keep innocence and take heed unto the thing that is right.
For that shall bring a man peace at the Last. Psm. 37 v. 38

Eighth Letter

Brit. Exped. Forces. Belgium
In-the-Trenches
10 Aug 1915

My darling Mother,

My best and fondest love for your birthday and may you have very many happy 'Returns of the Day'. I trust, Mother Darling, you will spend a happy day and I shall think of you at Home, my prayer being that God will shower down upon you his richest blessings for many years to come, and that soon he will grant unto this world a blessed peace and that he will restore me safely unto you in joy and peace. How I yearn Mother darling for that joyful day when I shall, if it be God's gracious will, return to my happy home, which God has richly blessed me with. I trust that you and all are enjoying the best of health. I am quite well and the cut is healing fast. I was charmed with yours and Mary's welcome letters which arrived last night.

I hope your visit to K'bro' will be accompanied by a spell of fine weather. I have had letters from Flo, Madi and Queenie Sharp today. Please send a carriage candle in my parcels in future as they are very hard to get here. Oh, Capt. Sowerby has been appointed to the Brigade staff as Capt. and he will not get any trench work now and a much nicer and safer job. I had a chat with him yesterday and he is very well. He goes to his new post today – the best of luck to him. Give my kindest regards to Mr., Mrs. and Miss Sowerby and I trust they are all well.

We had another heavy thunder rain yesterday which has made the trenches like "Venice". I met some fellows I knew in Oswald Tennant's Regt. He was shot through the back whilst adjusting his machine gun parapet, as he was in a stooping position.

I enclose a label from a Lemonade box. This brand is delicious and the best approach to real Lemon Juice. Could you get any – do you think? Florence likes Newport but the weather is wretched there. No doubt she will enjoy herself.

I suppose you received my letters last Sunday and Thursday. I am just enjoying a Thirstlet as it is very hot and they are very refreshing. I must close now Mother darling as I have just time for the mail. I hope you are all well at home. I expect a letter from Dad tomorrow.

Well good-bye Mother darling for the present. Wishing you all the joys of a birthday and with the blessing of our Heavenly Father, that for many years to come he will bless you with health, peace and many other of his bountiful blessings. My fondest love and kisses to you all and Mizpah.

Believe me, Mother darling.
Ever your loving Son,
Arthur G Wilson
Xxxxxxxxxxxxx

(On the back of the above letter is written
"My Birthday letter
From my Darling Boy
Aug the 18th 1915"

Memoirs

Our spell in the trenches continued throughout the summer. We had many casualties and I lost several gallant friends. On one occasion we were 36 days holding an advanced position without relief. We were under constant mortar and rifle grenade fire, the latter being a lethal and devastating weapon of immense power. It could not be seen or heard, only sometimes a strange thud could be heard when the weapon was fired – a vague and anxious warning.

29 1 87
(Extract of a letter written when he was 93)

Very dearest Rosemary and Michael,

I have just received the report on the last Armistice Celebration of the 2nd Battle of Ypres from Colin who has just rung me up in connection of our "proposed" visit to the special 70th anniversary of "The Battle of Passchendaele". If I am well enough I look forward VERY MUCH to be taking you as my guest to show you where I had a ghastly 8 months in 1915 (April to November) 2nd Battle of Ypres, and also where I was flying over the incredible Battle areas in 1917 with Bertie Sutton at 7 Squadron from September to the New Year of 1918. Now dear just ponder on this incredible thought – as it will be marvellous to show you where I lived in trenches deep in mud, all those months and under constant pressure from deadly German Snipers. I will be greatly moved to show you over these sacred realms.

NOTE: This letter refers to a trip organised by the dynamic historian Lyn Macdonald for veterans of World War 1. My father went on several of these trips which gave him great joy. I was his "Minder" on two of them. To witness the scenes and memorials of so much terrible slaughter was deeply moving – it took me a couple of months to recover from the wounding of my psyche.

Ninth Letter

This letter was probably written in August/September 1915, first two pages missing.
Page 3 starts:

Since the last family letter I have had the most thrilling episodes of my life, having been in the trenches and during the whole of our stay therein we have been either shelled or I have been on other work between the two firing lines. I was so delighted when the --- Regt. came and relieved us, as I had had enough for one spell – When I attempted to sleep the noise of the cannons was awful and I eagerly listened to see if any of these terrible shells fell near my dugout. I have had several exciting near shaves and some large shells fell very near to me. The trench mortars are wretched things and you can see them coming and then you rush the way opposite to where you think they will fall and quickly find cover behind the nearest parapet – Then a terrific roar and the whiz of Shrapnel through the air – a second more and all is over. The next thing to do is to see if the wretched shell has found any human targets.

I have also had some thrilling long hours in a Sap and wire mending. However thank God I am well and quite enjoying the slight rest from the nerve strain. How I rejoiced when I slung my heavy burden upon my shoulders and wended my way towards a safer zone. I thanked my God heartily for his blessings unto me, that he had delivered me from the terrible dangers which always exist in the firing line. I well know that all my past slight trials and hardships will be nothing in comparison to the trials which are before me and before the victory will be ours in this terrible war – I cannot in future mention the war in my letters – or anything about it.*

(* Due to strict censoring of all letters. I don't know how he got away with such graphic descriptions!)

Thanks so much for the Cigs. etc and the apples which were lovely. I never enjoyed an apple better in my life. I say, you have not sent me the Cigarette. case Reg gave to me – it was in the large box from Sutton-on-Sea – I wish you would send it next parcel please please, it is small and will not take up much valuable room in my pocket.[4] Thanks very much for the "P.C.s". You will be pleased to hear that I have just written to Mrs Richardson, Margaret, S.A. Smith, Uncle George (Melbourne) and Aunt Jennie – Quite a colossal mail n'est ce pas. I hope Mother darling you received my letter yesterday with the N.Z. mail and the Silk Card and the Photo. I know you will forgive the hasty note as we were on the move and I was just lucky enough to scrape a hasty message. I hope you will like the card which was hand done by a Refugee, which I sent specially for you as I think it is lovely, don't you? Now the photo is a souvenir which hope you will <u>keep</u> as it has a <u>very</u> unique history – which I cannot relate here – notice the bullet mark near the top. I hope to send dear Auntie a silk post card in a few days. I was so

---

4 This was for keeping the cigarettes dry from the incessant rain and damp clothing.

delighted to receive her kind letter, but sorry to hear of poor Evie's husband's illness.

Now Pater dear, I am sorry to read about your teeth troubles and hope that by now you are well again.. Yes I fear the hay crops will be very scanty in England – you are lucky to have two good stacks. I hope you get a good figure for your surplus hay. The crops here are fine and so thick.

Now darling Girls – How do you like the Scarlet Pimpernels?[5] I sent 4 pieces so that you all could have one each, besides I gathered them within a 1/4 of a mile from the Germans – so they ought to interest you. I have just had a letter from Mrs. Sharp and a lovely parcel from my dear friends at 26A. Yes Mother I get a nice letter every few days from --- who is going to Harrogate with Mrs Hunt for some time – I hope this visit will restore Mrs Hunt to good health – she has been ill for 6 months now. I hope Mr Rees received my letter written from the trenches about 4 days ago. I am so pleased, Barbie pet, that the garden is looking so well and that the inhabitants of the Greenhouse are such a success. I will also try and send all you Girls one of the Silk P.Cards. Has Mr Rees seen the Souvenirs and do you like them? What do you think of the German Helmet? I had another lovely box ready addressed and when I took it to the Orderly Room it was refused – much to my utter disappointment, as all parcels from the front are now barred as the weight is getting tremendous. No wonder says I *!!!* I also wrote to Gladys in Northampton so most of my friends got a letter before the Letter Act comes into force. I regret that this act has been brought in so I can only write home once a week – but don't mind, I will let you have a card or letter as often as I possibly can.

Well, my darling ones, how are you all? I am so glad Madi is so much better. Well Edith will be with you now at glorious Ashtree House. How I wish I were there too – Anyhow I hope to be there soon.

I pray that you all should receive the richest blessings which our heavenly Father graciously bestows upon his elect. May his Holy Spirit be poured upon you all and strengthen, cheer and abide with you all through this mortal life of trouble and sorrow. God grant that my earnest prayer will be answered that very soon he will restore me safely home to you in peace – What joy will be mine – No one will be happier than I! What ceaseless praises I shall be blessed to utter and with what joy shall I go towards the Altar of God in our dear little parish Church and there pour out my earnest prayers and adoring praises to my Blessed Redeemer.

Well goodbye for a few days and with my fondest love and kisses to you all and with the abiding presence of our dear Lord, which I pray links me to my dear home in true and faithful unity.

---

5 *Scarlet Pimpernels – I think these must have been wild flowers, also known as Shepherd's Barometer and Poor Man's Weatherglass. The plant has had a reputation for medicinal use for several hundred years, being prescribed as a herbal remedy for ailments as diverse as melancholy, epilepsy and gout!*

Someone wrote   "No heart can think, no tongue can tell The virtues of the Pimpernel".

Au'revoir au present and Mizpah.
Believe me,
Ever your true and most loving Son and brother
A G WILSON
PS: Some more Soap and Razor (hand), toothpaste and Cig. Case in large box from Sutton.

Written on the back of the final page of letter 9:-

Verses 4 & 5

> I feel sustained. I am sustained, my Lord
> And Why, Because I'm trusting in thy word.
> Thou said'st it, yet I ne'er before could see
> That Thou was speaking just alone TO ME.
>
> Now dearest Lord of Thee I ask no more
> Than that Thou wilt, until this life is o'er
> Thus prove each day the mysteries of Thy Grace
> Until mine eyes shall see Thee face to face.

Finis

> Holy Father in Thy mercy
> Hear my anxious prayer.
> Keep our loved ones, now far absent,
>   'Neath Thy care.
>
> Draw nigh to God and he will draw nigh to you.
> James iv 8v

MIZPAH
AGW
XXXXXXX

These passages from Peter's memoirs give a useful insight into life with the West Yorks at this time:

One day, when walking along the canal bank, I observed the Brigadier, his monocle fixed in his eye, very diligently going through the seams of his shirt and dealing with the alien lice who had taken up residence in his garment. He seemed to be having a good harvest and I passed along leaving him in "full cry".

And:

All August in trenches – many casualties and several friends killed, being on wiring parties and subject to counter-bombardments. Very frequent heavy rains and trenches very muddy. Had to share gum boots when on duty as some troops suffered from trench feet. (The whole foot and toes become swollen and inflamed and wearing gum boots made the condition worse – very painful and it was impossible to march.) Had several parties with Jimmy Ogden (member of the Harrogate Jewellers Firm) who had a succession of sensational food parcels.

Very heavy rains late August and September – mud and water in the trenches over tops of gumboots, which had to be shared during duty spells when guarding parapets. Heavy bombardments often caused trenches and dugouts to collapse and some troops suffocated when overcome with fatigue and when sleeping in lightly built dugouts which fell in upon troops.

I found two splendid members of the Norfolk Regiment had died during sleep and only in a small dugout which collapsed upon them with no evidence of wounds. The earth had fallen in upon them and they were suffocated and had only been dead a few hours."

And another extract:

"I had several walks through Ypres and saw the tremendous destruction and devastation caused by months of relentless German bombardments. During all the late summer and autumn we were holding a long stretch of the front line and under constant German bombardment and even when in reserve positions, when we were resting, casualties continued to mount. At "stand-to", which was the period approaching dawn, when all ranks manned the front line, our position, being in the advanced front of the Ypres Salient, was subject to sniper fire and we suffered many casualties. There were several large trees which had been totally destroyed by the months of heavy shell fire and German snipers were crafty and skilful in constructing a sniper point in the shattered branches. It was when dawn was breaking they entered these posts, and with the accurate rifle fitted with a telescopic sight, watched over sections of our trenches and waited for a victim as they came into the deadly sight of this lethal weapon. We were only 200 yards away from the German front line which was protected by belts of heavy barbed wire entanglements: it almost followed the contour and was usually well above our trench system. The enemy were able to pump out the water which accumulated in

their trenches and directed the flow down the slope. During long spells of rain we had to face this added discomfort. The German snipers never used the same sniper post more than a few times and were probably 500 to 600 yards away.

On one occasion I had a very near shave as, enthroned on a solitary latrine, a sniper's bullet crashed into the latrine bucket a few inches below my torso with a mighty thud. I jumped into action without delay and sought the cover and protection of the main trench to escape a further shot. The latrine was promptly moved to another site, well protected with heavily massed sandbags and totally beyond the view of any German observation post. I often attended to the wounded and assisted the regular stretcher bearers in helping to carry casualties to the forward dressing stations."

There was a poignant moment in November 1987, when my father and I visited Ypres with Lyn Macdonald and her veterans. My father participated in the wonderful ceremony of remembrance at the Menin Gate. The local fire brigade buglars, as they do daily, played The Last Post.

Some idea of the ferocity of the battles can be gleaned from the fact no fewer than 54,896 names are inscribed at the memorial. These represent only those brave British and Commonwealth lads who have no known grave, their shattered bodies strewn around the adjacent battlefields. And near Thiepval on the Somme where Peter was wounded is another memorial which commemorates 74000 young men with no known grave, an unbearable thought.

Tenth Letter

Brit Ex Forces, Belgium
16th Sunday after Trinity
19 9 15

"I desire that ye faint not at my tribulations for you which is your glory. For this cause I bow my knees unto the Father of our Lord Jesus Christ." Ephes.iii 13v

My dearest Parents and all,

It is a glorious Sabbath here and I have just finished my dinner which consisted of skilly, which was really remarkable by its resemblance to washing up water! The whole last 11 days have been gloriously fine, a splendid stroke of luck for all us Tommies during this rest, which terminates tomorrow. The lasting spell of fine weather has enabled me to enjoy my outdoor life in this Bivouac. I sleep like a top in the pure air and I don't feel the cold a bit. If rain had fallen I'm afraid I should have had some exciting and depressing times, however good luck has rested upon me and here I am as happy as a Highland Shepherd, sitting just outside the Bivy, with a cooling breeze wafting past and the sun is glorious. I fear this letter will be shorter than usual as nothing of interest has been happening – Every day has been like the other. I will do my best to supply you all with some notes which I hope will interest you.

I must first thank you for the various letters etc. which charmed me. Barbie's last letter was lovely and was so deeply interesting. I expect a letter from Mother darling and Mary tonight as the mail was suspended yesterday. Oh! The parcel has not yet arrived although I received your letter dear Pater two days ago, which should have arrived with the parcel.

Yesterday we held Brigade Boxing Tournaments and there was large quantities of blood flying about, but notwithstanding the fact that the men had had no training, the boxing was first rate. The excitement was intense all through and the punching was huge – almost every bout was a knockout. I have had two matches of Rugger against the 7th and 8th Battalions Leeds Rifles. The match against the 8th was great. Three men were carried off and 5 out of our team, including myself had our shirts torn completely off. I was skinned like a Rabbit with about 3 fellows of the Rifles round my leg, neck and body! Notwithstanding the fact that I was thus left only clothed with a pair of pants cut short, which supplied me with the footer breeches, I continued until the end of the great game which resulted in a win for the gallant 5th by 1 try to nil. The heat was awful and everyone was done and perspiration rolled off us all. We also have had some very jolly concerts supplied by a party of artists which travel at the front and supply concerts at Rest camps.

I hope the cash and the lace Belgian collar for Barbie arrived safely. I will now surprise you all or rather make you laugh. I am drinking BEER – but the liquor is not intoxicating. The water here is very scarce and impure and the heat is awful. I drank a little water which repeatedly gave me acute pains of terrible consequence in my stomach. I was told to take some Belgian beer which is a National drink here and is made in every house. I did so and never had any pains as before.

It is so funny to see even Belgian babies and children drinking this beer in large quantities. The people here do not drink tea. I hope you will not think I am a drunkard and a slave to drink, as this stuff is really a medicine as well as a beverage. We have several men in hospital with sickness caused through the consumption of the impure water. I have drunk water which looked filthy from shell holes and pools but I feel none of the worse so far. Oh please send me a tin of Boots Vaime. The Jaspers are still very active and ferocious.

I have again had the blessed privilege of attending the celebration of the Holy Communion this morning and hope to go again tomorrow morning as the Chaplain has offered to conduct a final celebration before our departure to the trenches tomorrow. We are going to a very hot part of the line and may be ages before we return to civilization, or have an opportunity of partaking in that blessed service. You, my dearest ones at home, cannot possibly realize how dear and blessed these celebrations are to me out here. They surpass the home service, possibly it is because God is so near to me here and recently he has bestowed upon me many secret and rich blessings.

Just at this moment the band is playing in the forest and it sounds lovely and so cheering. I am quite impressed to read that you have got all my goods from Knaresborough. I don't want any warmer clothes yet, if possible I will go through the winter without them. Ever so pleased the garden is so lovely and that the fruit etc is such a success. I am delighted the weather has favoured Auntie and Uncle for their holidays. I expect by this time they will be back again at Clodagh. Oh mother dear what do you think to the little souvenir ring?

Monday Morn. 20 9 15: I was delighted to receive the glorious parcel which arrived safely. The grapes were lovely and as fresh and firm as if just cut. The spearmints were glorious and the cakes and potted meat were delicious. The peach was, much to my delight, in good condition and was eagerly devoured. I also received by the same mail Mother's P.C. and Mary's letter and was delighted to read that Barbie likes the collar. I hoped to go to P., a large town near here, today but we are ordered to the trenches tonight, so our rest will be shorter than we expected. However we are in fine spirits and ready for what comes along.

We are marching to the trenches for a 24 day spell in fighting order. All our packs will be left behind, so I will have a beard like a Greek when I return, if God spares me – I shall have no kit at all with me so please excuse lack of correspondence if such should occur. We are going to a hot part of the line and as you see by the papers, this front is very angry and the cannonade is fierce. I expect my shirt etc. will be in a lovely condition when I return but that's a mere detail - needless to say I shall look forward to my weekly parcel and lovely letters from my dear home with great eagerness and joy.

The celebration this morning was too real to comment upon and the clergyman was an O.P. *(old boy of St Peter's School, York)* and called Whincup, Mrs Whincup's Brother-in-Law. Only 7 attended in that corner of the forest and when we bowed our heads on bended knees and the solemn and divine words of God's blessing came forth, the Holy Spirit of God seemed to descend mightily upon us, and all were compelled to admit that the divine presence of our Blessed Redeemer was earnestly felt. Thus we left that blessed service by committing our Souls and Bodies unto our divine Creator, trusting him that in his mercy he would watch over us and protect us until this awful war is o'er: or in divine and perfect submission to his holy will, that he would fit us for his blessed presence in peace. I said with a heart full of faith and confidence in my God "I will go forth from strength to strength and make mention of His righteousness only." I can gladly say that I return tonight to the line with joy and a thankful heart that God has permitted me to fight against our wicked foe for the honour of my King, country and dear home. I had a long chat with the Chaplain who was delighted to meet me.

I have had a glorious rest and feel as fit as ever and no rain has fallen during our rest, which has been ideal. Well my dearest ones, I must close as we are moving now and I have to look after my section. I trust you are all well and happy and I trust that Mother darling and dear Aunt feel that K. has done them both much good.

Unto Him that is able to do exceedingly abundantly above what we ask and think, I commit you all ………. Well good-bye dear ones for a few days and my fondest love and kisses to you all. MIZPAH.
Believe me,
Your ever loving Son,
Arthur G Wilson
Xxxxxx

For he shall give his Angels charge over Thee, to keep thee in all thy ways.
Psalms xci v.xi

Eleventh Letter

British Ex Force
In-the-Trenches
18ᵗʰ Sunday after Trinity
3 10.1915

"Waiting for the coming of our Lord Jesus Christ who shall also confirm you unto the end, that ye may be blameless in the day of our Lord Jesus Christ." 1 Cor. 1 Chap. Verse vi

My dearest Parents and all,

The first Sabbath in October has dawned upon this world of tumult and unrest: and thank God during the last week we have been blessed with a glorious victory. I need not disclose to you any details of the battles, as I know the English papers will be busy relating to all the joyful people of dear England. I can only say we are still doing splendidly. I pray, that through the grace of our divine Capt. that soon He will give unto the gallant Allies the glorious victory which will lead to a lasting peace. I pray that after peace has been graciously restored that many may come forward to enlist in the armies of the Living God and offer their lives for their God and for his blessed service.

Our spell in the front line has been very lively and real, also the rain has been most troublesome during the greater part of the period. At present I am in reserve a few hundred yards from the firing line. We left the firing line last night and I am at this moment sat in a lovely little dugout overlooking the famous Canal. The bullets are still coming over with a merry whiz! And in reserve you all get shelled as it is favourable for the enemy. The firing line is only 100-200 yards apart and in parts where we have been, you can say "good morning" to our Hun foes as the distance is only 25 yards apart. This part of the line is famous for bombing and I can throw a hand bomb 40 yards.

At last I have seen my feet which I find alright, but rather sore. The trenches were very muddy and plenty of water about and my feet have been wet through during the whole of the spell. Consequently my feet became sore as I had not had my boots off for days. The soles were very red and the pain was like a burn. However last night I had the great pleasure of taking my wet boots and socks off and after a good rub with O'Kirby's salve the pain was greatly relieved and this morning they are much better – I hope tomorrow morn will see them in perfect trim. Kirby is quite fit and sends his usual wishes.

I was on duty part of every night in the trenches and as usual it rained during the greater part of my watch. The nights were very dark and I had to pace about frequently to keep my wet feet warm. It was a great comfort to me during those long, lonely hours to realize that the divine presence of my dear Lord was always with me – my communions with Him were real. I really can say that I felt as if God himself was with me.

There was one place where a fallen British hero lay buried with a small wooden cross marking his last earthly resting place. I offered many prayers near that spot, so sad and yet so glorious ("Greater love hath no man, than to lay down his life for his friends"), whilst around me the air was full of the roar of the battle and the cracking of bullets. That little section of God's Acre seemed to appeal to me as sacred in that field of battle. I frequently found myself there during the night watches with my heavenly Capt. waiting to receive my petitions and to grant unto me that strength and courage which no earthly source can bestow. You, dear ones at home, cannot realize how great a source of joy and comfort my blessed Redeemer is to me during this awful conflagration. He says above the roar of the battle "Be of good cheer I have overcome the world."

We haven't half had some of "Krupps Selected"[6] during the last spell – the roar of the guns must have been heard for miles and miles. I have seen several Huns this last week and spent some time sniping through a borrowed sniper's post. My glasses, which I had borrowed, were ripping and I brought some of the Hun faces right close – I could see their teeth. We were quite close to the Huns and they seemed very ratty when they received the news of their keen defeat. They hurled at us every description of their clever war weapons and we spent quite an exciting time dodging trench mortars and taking cover from shells.

One of our Airmen went over the German lines and the sky was like a fly paper filled with flies, compared to the number of shells they fired at him. It was marvellous how he lived in such a fire – he came back calmly and we gave him a ringing cheer. Our airmen often go over their lines and seem to have complete mastery of the air. If a Hun plane comes within range, he is soon seeking the nearest way back to his lines as our Anti Aircraft batteries are fine and accurate. Just as I sit now looking through the dugout door the sun is commencing to set and the sky is perfect. One of our gallant airmen is busy patrolling and his propeller is buzzing like a swarm of bees. It may interest you to know that Jack Frost is conspicuous by his presence just now – quite a change - Eh!

Now I must find words in order to thank you for the lovely parcel which arrived in perfect condition. I had just come from the front line and it was getting late – as usual I felt hungry and retired to my dugout. I was preparing my KIP for the night (which is the soldier for bed) when one of my gallant section roared out "Cpl. Wilson. I've two parcels for you". I was overjoyed and eagerly opened the parcel from "Home Sweet Home". If you had been here unseen in the dugout and beheld the joy and emotion caused by your lovely parcel, I am sure tears would have rolled down your cheeks, your hearts would have been touched so. The cakes which first met my eye caused quite a roar of vocal joy and the other cake was met with a similar reception. I can only say I

---

6 *a reference to the huge German Armament manufacturer*

feel most grateful to you dear ones for your kindness in sending me such lovely parcels. The eggs were so nice and the toffee is fine. Thanks so much for the scissors and the shaving soap etc. The other parcel was from Miss Norcross and it contained a glorious assortment of pears, apples, oranges, bananas and tomatoes, which much to my joy, arrived in perfect condition. I had a lovely supper which was followed by me laying down beneath my blanket and with a thankful heart I offered up to my bounteous Lord my thanksgivings for sending me such a glorious gift of food, and after committing myself to His divine charge I fell into a much needed sleep.

It will no doubt interest you when I tell you that I slept last night with only my shirt on – it was a real treat to kick off my trousers, socks etc. The only drawback was the cold night and this morning early I was like an iceberg. However, notwithstanding the cold, I had a fine sleep. I will now break off for tea exit.

It is now 8.30 pm and I will continue with this epistle for you, my dearest ones. I must thank you Barbara dear for your lovely long letter which arrived, to my great joy, two nights ago. It was a lovely construction and full of interesting phrases. My dear, I love to peruse your ever welcome Sunday epistle – Methinks that even now at this very moment your pen is beating time with mine – you will be busy writing that treasured letter to me.

Hullo! Bang. Thud! Bang!!. The Huns have just sent over some huge shells right near here – the noise of the mighty explosions is like countless thunderstorms. It is quite easy to hear the pieces of shell and shrapnel splash with thuds as they strike the water of the Canal. You can also hear the pieces of shell strike the ruined trees around here. I think the German Officers must be having a walk round their guns and have told the gunners to send a few Krupps Specials over to let us know they are alive and well and still have a few shells, which our Tommies call "Iron Rations".

This morning I was put on a mining fatigue, just my luck for the Sabbath day, however as luck would have it, I struck oil. Off I marched with my gallant party to the specified place. I soon found the Officer who I had to report to. To my joy he said "I shall not require you this morning, Corpl. as I have some other business". Of course I did not discuss any details but was eager to get away before the officer altered his welcome decision. After a few words I saluted him and eagerly retraced my steps to the men, who I had left standing a few yards away. I ordered them to "Quick March" and they thought I was leading them to the mining place. When near the dugouts I said that we had struck oil and that they could all fall out as our labours were not required this morning. Thus with smiles upon all our faces we marched away to our various dugouts feeling quite pleased with ourselves.

Ah! I hear sounds of the mail – yes and another huge parcel from you dear ones at home and 6 letters. I have got nearly half of the platoon's mail. I must have a few seconds grace so as to investigate this most welcome arrival. The letters are ……….

Mr Smith's is killing, he is a sport – I am glad he is fit enough to join the gallant Australians.

You girls had a nice afternoon at the Elms – I am so glad my wounded chums had an enjoyable afternoon. I say you would feel disappointed when the wounded soldiers failed to present themselves for tea. I hope next time you will have a happy sit down. Now a word about the parcel – All I can say is – I thank you with all my heart for the glorious contents which have arrived in perfect condition. The fruit is lovely, and the grapes are now before me suspended from a nail as fresh as if hanging on my vine. I am at present busily engaged in the consumption of a Pearmain[7] which is delicious and one of my comrades is greatly enjoying the other. I am so pleased you have sent the milk, as now I can enjoy the Quaker Oats beyond measure. The candles will do A1 and I will take care with them. I am at present writing this in candle light and every few minutes the outer darkness is illuminated with the rockets sent up from the firing line. The grapes are lovely, so sweet; all here greatly admire and enjoy them.

Auntie from Clodagh says that her visit to Haxby was ideal and both feel much better for the change. They were both delighted with the garden and especially with the souvenirs. I say these grapes are lovely – I keep pulling one off the bunch every few sentences. I do not wish my parcels to be costly, as I know most goods at home have risen immensely and I must go short. Plain eatables will be greatly appreciated and the parcels need not be so large thus saving a little in postage. I am so pleased the grapes went to help to adorn the altar of God at the harvest Festival – I always like the best bunch to be given to the Lord. I hope you had a good service and a large congregation.

I think your plan Barbie dear for the Sunday School Hymn Books is splendid, I feel sure they will look nice. I hope the Vicar likes them. I am delighted Capt. Sowerby has given you another call, yes he is very lucky to get on leave a second time. Some other officers here have been on leave for the 2nd time, but us poor tommies must wait patiently and we will wait too. I am feeling very well and can tackle anything now – I don't think I have ever felt better. I was quite delighted to meet Lt Breace whom I know very well and Hamilton, that fine Irish boy who is in the Motor Machine Gun Section.

Now I should be greatly obliged if you would send my next parcel to a comrade who is greatly neglected. Nobody writes to him and he never gets a parcel. I feel so sorry for him and he always gets a very welcome share from my parcels. His address is Pte. C. Carter 3021 16 Platoon D Co. 1/5 W. Yks. B.E.F. France. The poor fellow is also unable to write and has been seriously neglected at home. I do not mean that you have to send me a parcel, it is to be the one you send weekly for me which I desire to be sent

---

7 *A pear*

to Carter.[8] He has 5 other brothers serving and a father.

Well my dearest ones. I must stop for tonight as it is now 10 pm and I am feeling tired – I will finish this in the morning. I will close my eyes this night with the joy of knowing that I am in His own safe keeping and I pray that He will bring me safely unto another day. Good night!!

Monday morning has dawned and to our slight disappointment it is raining with great force – I have just finished a lovely breakfast which consisted of "Quaker oats avec Lait et Sucre", Bacon etc. I am sat under the cover of my Dugout, which so far has proved to be waterproof. I had a glorious sleep last night and was quite warm. The powder has committed great havoc amongst the Jaspers and I feel much relieved from their attacks. This shirt, which has clothed me for the last month, is completely soaked with Boots powder and I hope to get another clean shirt in about 3 weeks time. When a shirt is worn over a month and you get wet through every few nights you can probably imagine the condition of one of our Grey Backs in the final stages. Behold, there is a fatigue party passing just now and all the mud underneath makes the transport of heavy loads difficult. I am glad I was detailed for yesterday morning's fatigue, which luckily was cancelled. It is marvellous what weights some of the Tommies can carry. I will now give you a short description of an engineer's fatigue on a soaking wet night in muddy Trenches.

On the command "*advance*" we pick up our loads which are tremendous . The nights are very dark and the first thing that generally happens is, you slip or put your feet into an unseen hole. Down you go bang Wallop!! After getting up all plastered with wet mud you proceed whilst the air is full of cruel phrases of an awful nature concerning the miserable Kaiser. The greatest nuisance is the frequent halts which are caused by various means and when one is bearing a very heavy and awkward load the whole affair is miserable. Of course, we know the work has to be done so we don't really mind and look forward to the time when we shall be retracing our steps towards our dugouts, which when we arrive are generally swimming with water which has penetrated the earth roof. After about an hour's trudge we arrive at our destination , work for a few hours and then after satisfying our officers, we move for home. During the whole time bullets etc are whizzing past and we frequently have a casualty. Bullets somehow don't seem to worry us to any extent, they whizz past and frequently come uncommonly near, but as long as they don't find us as a target, we carry on. If a fellow gets hit it's a mere stroke of luck to the Huns as they cannot possibly see us. So we return in quite good spirits and the N.C.O. in charge sees that we are all present and then we all slide off to our dugouts. We don't bother to remove our wet clothes or mud but lay down on our oilsheet and with our Top Coat to cover us, we soon enter the "Land of Nod".

I should like you to send me a Razor case for the Wheatsheaf as I have worn the

---

8 *I tried via those wonderful people, the Commonwealth War Graves Commission, to find out if Pte. C. Carter had been killed. A shocking statistic was forthcoming: There are no fewer than 114 C. Carters among the war dead. Happily none of these bears No. 3021, so maybe my father's friend survived.*

cardboard one out. Marks & Spencer have a useful wooden case which will do A1. Please forward a P.O. for 15/- to Uncle Wal at your convenience, in payment of a watch, which he kindly obtained and sent out to me. I also received the welcome letter from Beckett & Co.[9], which comes at the end of every quarter. It is now 11 a.m. and the rain seems to have cleared off. I hope it will not return for a lengthy season. But alas the wet season approaches. Thus we must expect rough weather. I am delighted the garden still looks well and the fruit crop must be wonderful. Now I must ask how you dear ones are getting on. I hope Mother darling you are still well and not worrying. Your last letter was the sweetest composition I have ever read – I often thank God for giving me such a good Christian home and parents. My joy too will be unbounded if God in his mercy preserves me to return "to my father's house in peace". I pray that that glad day will soon dawn and that England will be ringing forth with peals of bells from our countless glorious Cathedrals and Parish churches; Yea, God grant that before many more moons wax or wane this war will be a drama of the past and that the Dove of peace will forever abide in this sinful planet, which is a speck in the great and mysterious universe.

Well my dearest ones I fear I have tired you with this lengthy epistle of an extraordinary length. I am just going to have dinner so my comrade is preparing some Coffee au Lait and the Chicken which I know will be first class.

I commit you all unto the divine protection of our blessed Redeemer. May he in His mercy guide me safely through this terrible war and restore me safely unto you all in joy and peace, if it be His glorious will. If we meet not here again, I pray that as a family I may, with my dear Lord at my side, welcome you all at the Golden Gates of Eternity, where for ever in the divine presence of our loved Master we shall offer up unceasing praises before the Throne of God. The abiding love of our dear Lord be with you all. Good bye and Mizpah.

Believe me,
Ever your loving Son etc. XXXXXXXX
Arthur G Wilson, Cpl. B.E.F.

"Then we which are alive and remain shall be caught up together with them in the clouds to meet the Lord in the air and so shall we be ever with the Lord, wherefore comfort one another with these words." 1 Thess. 4 Chap. 17 & 18 verses.

(On back of this letter (which was 14 pages long!) is a P.S.:

My feet are better today, no soreness whatsoever. A.G.W.

---

9 Note: Becketts Bank for whom he was working in Knaresborough when he joined up.

Twelfth Letter

B. Ex. F. In-the-Trenches
19th Sunday after Trinity
10 10 1915

"And be ye kind one to another, tender-hearted, forgiving one another, even as God for Christ's sake hath forgiven you." Ephes. 11

My Dearest Parents,

I think I can say that this letter will have been written nearer to the Huns than any previously. We are only about 40 yards away from the Bosches and the space between us is one mass of barbed wire entanglements. The picture being almost like a mammoth spider's web.

You will notice this notepaper as that which you purchased so kindly for me in old York last week. It is part of the contents of your lovely parcel which arrived safely to my great joy this Sabbath morning. You will probably wonder why the parcel was two days late – Well on Friday night no parcels came to the trenches,so they all came up last night with the usual ration party. The fruit and tomatoes are as fresh as can be and the cakes etc look very tempting. I hope to enjoy some of the potted meat today, all being well. The candles will do A1 in these trenches and I am sticking to them like glue. It is quite a delicacy to have English cucumber and tomatoes in the firing line. I enjoyed the eggs for breakfast immensely and I thank you deeply for the lovely parcel.

I hope you will carry out the instructions for next week's parcel as requested in last Sunday's long letter. I have found out a new and splendid treatment for my friends the Jaspers. Will you please send me a tin of "Harrison's Pommard" in my next parcel – the price is 4½d at any Chemists. Now that the cold weather is approaching the "Js" cling on like leeches and are most active during the nights. You, my dear ones at home, cannot realise how much joy and comfort your treasured letters bring with them. Oh! I must tell you those soups which you so kindly sent to me are lovely – I made one boiling in my Dixie yesterday and the flavour was exquisite. The soup reminded me of dear Father's usual dish, which he so enjoys when he returns from the hunting field. I think I shall try some "Lentil" for dinner today, whilst I suppose you dear ones at home will be partaking of the fatted calf and Yorks. pudding! What does your office as Recruiting Officer include? Have you any uniform or badge to show your authority etc?

Just as I was about to prepare my breakfast this Sabbath morn – the dreaded words *"Stretcher Bearers at the Double"* sounded in my ears. Off I bolted in the direction of the sound, as the S. Bearers were a short distance away, and I knew I could attend to the casualty and do some good, in case the S. Bearers were delayed. I soon came to the place of the casualty – A beastly German sniper, not 50 yards away, had found his human target and the bullet struck the unfortunate fellow just a fraction of an inch above his left eye. The few fellows around seemed quite unable to attend the poor man – they were probably unable to attend the wounded as even many strong men are. I hastily placed the wounded man into a comfortable position and I knew if I stood erect – I could get potted as well – as the place was in a sap in advance of the firing line, (sandbagged up to shoulders) which is used as an advanced post. Having torn open the field dressing, I also applied some Iodine to the wound, which was a cruel gash and bled badly. I think the bullet must have scorched his eye, but I was delighted to think that the bullet had not penetrated his brain. By the time I had the bandage ready the S. Bearers came up and we soon had the wounded man on his way to the dressing station. The unlucky fellow seemed to be in fairly good spirit all things considered, but the Dr. thinks that he will lose his eye. I have had several experiences where it has been necessary to render 1st Aid immediately, as the S.B.s may be engaged on other casualties quite near.

Hullo: Fritz – There is a German sniper who keeps hitting these sandbags and I cannot see his object –he doesn't half scatter the earth. Go on Fritz – We can hear the Huns mock and shout near here and with the glasses I can see a cross which marks the resting place of some fallen Huns. I cannot make out what the words inscribed are. The cross is painted white and worded in black. *(Diagram was drawn here of the cross-shape(complex.)*

I have been potting at a fellow who has been using a mallet this morning …I am also enjoying some of the lovely pears, the flavour is lovely. You must have a wonderful fruit crop and the wounded will be delighted to receive your appreciated consignments. Fancy comparing our two present situations. You and your S. School scholars are at this moment offering up prayers and thanksgivings in our dear little Parish Church. I am just behind the trenches and the ground is trembling before the explosions of mighty shells – the bombardment is in progress on the right. The weather is very fine for this part of the season and I hope that the rain will keep off for a good time yet.

It is quite news to read that Uncle Alfred is once again at Haxby. I wonder if Major Bullogh is going on foreign service. I see his wife has returned to the stage and is devoting her salary to Military charities. Fancy it is over six months since I parted at Gainsboro and left the dear old chalk cliffs of England. It was a great comfort to me when we parted at Gainsbro. to find that you, my dearest parents, said good-bye with such a good heart. You well knew my destination – you knew it was my duty to go and fight by the side of my brave brother comrades against our unmanly foe. I am proud to think that God has permitted me to fight for my dear country. When I last beheld your dear faces and said good-bye – my earnest prayer from that moment until now has been "that God in His love and mercy would spare me to see again those whom I love at home. God grant that even that glad day may not be far distant and that very soon a glorious victory will be ours, which will be the forerunner of a righteous and lasting peace throughout this world.

Well I must now ask – How are all you dear ones at home? I suppose Florence and Eddie have the usual heated discussions during the homework session. I hope both will receive rosy reports at half term – How do the souvenirs look – and has the Vicar seen them yet? I got a lovely helmet the other day and was so sorry I could not send it home, as the sending of souvenirs is now unlawful according to the Law of the Medes and Persians!

I enclose herewith two souvenirs which are made by a tommy in this Regt. from French bullets. I think they are sweet and if dipped in gold they would make a nice neat pendant (whatever you call it)!! I don't know who's turn it is for souvenirs, but you will know – if you would all like one (I mean the feminine members of the family), I would love to send you one each as I have ten on order. I hope you will like them and I should like to know if they arrive in safety, as many letters are opened now.

I think I must draw to a close as it is post time. Please give my best wishes to all my inquiring friends and say I am in the pink.

May God ever watch over you all and may He, in His redeeming love, grant me a safe return home, to you my dearest ones in health and peace, is the unceasing prayer of –
Ever your loving Son. MIZPAH
Arthur G Wilson, Cpl.
Xxxxxxx
B.E.F.
10 10 15

"Lo I am with you always
Even unto the end of the world." Matt.

Thirteenth Letter

B.E.F. Belgium
In-the-Trenches
21st Sunday after Trinity

"My brethren, be strong in the Lord, and in the power of his might. Put on the whole armour of God, that ye may be able to stand against the wiles of the devil." Ephes. vi.10

My dearest Parents and all,

Once again the ceaseless din of battle is ringing in my ears and I am in the trenches ready for any duty whatever it may be. The leaves are falling fast from the shattered trees of devastated Belgium and the whole district looks dismal. Even the birds have departed from our midst; the only living creatures of nature are rats which infest every square yard of earth. They exist in hordes and as soon as the sun sinks the whole place becomes alive with countless numbers of this unpleasant class of vermin; they utter very weird noises and dart about investigating the piles of rubbish until the welcome dawn approaches this barren and war stricken part of God's earth.

Our REST was a keen disappointment to us all; really we are better off in the trenches as during the whole period we were constantly working and had no time whatever to ourselves. Just before departing for the trenches I was on my way back to REST billet, wending my way alone, yet not alone, through hop fields. I was returning from a special celebration of the blessed sacrament which was a glorious service. A ruined barn was the "House of God" and therein I partook of those sacred emblems with a heart full of thankfulness to my Almighty Father for bestowing such an unspeakable gift upon me. There, before that sacred and divine presence, I offered up my petitions to my Redeemer beseeching Him that in His mercy He would go forth with me into the battle to fight, not only against earthly foes, but from those deep and spiritual foes,which prevail with tremendous domination in our daily life out here. My joy was great when I heard that before departing to the scene of battle, I should have an opportunity of holding another divine service at such a needful time. Thus I left that glorious service with the assurance that God was with me and I uttered these words "I shall go forth in the strength of the Lord God and will make mention of His righteousness only". My heart was full of joy as I returned and the divine courage, which God has given me, is a great source of strength to me on this campaign. Though only our Major and myself from our Battln. attended, the service was divine.

The transport was to have taken part of our kit, but just at the last moment the order came "Men will carry all their kit". If you could have seen me you would have thought I was a camel laden with baggage! The weight was terrific, but after over three long hours we arrived at the trenches and not one of the Gallant Fifth fell out – a really fine achievement, n'est ce pas? The moon shone brightly: that did not lighten our loads, but it certainly made our march more cheerful. The fellows sang with a spirit of enthusiasm, which I feel sure does not exist with the Bosches just over the other side of "No Man's Land". The men were soon down in the reserve trenches and only a few seconds found those off duty fast asleep. We found that water would be wanted for tomorrow's meal, so Lee – Sgt. Kirby and myself, who are in charge of the platoon, and another Tommy declared that we would go for water. Off we went as we could not entertain the thought of disturbing our weary comrades. After roaming about we came to a desolate house, which had been reduced to the ground by shell fire. Here we found a well and by the aid of some wire and a bucket we obtained enough water for our comrades for the morrow. Several bullets came over, but we succeeded in reaching our trenches in safety – we could not be seen but during the dark hours a sharp rifle fire is always kept up, and often a bullet finds its target. We had one man hit coming into trenches, just in front of me, by a bullet, but not serious. He was over a mile from the firing line.

I had just got into my dugout and was almost asleep, when the telephone man came and said we had to send a party for rations. So I got up and took the party and we went to a ruined village which was in an awful state. We passed patches of ground which were crowded with little wooden crosses, showing that beneath rested the bodies of many gallant comrades who had given their lives for their country's sake. There they lay, with their faces towards their foes, against whom they have so bravely fought – also facing the celestial gates of Eternity, They rest there in that lovely section of God's acre with their blanket around them, waiting for the Angel to sound the Last Trumpet, which I pray will summon them all to the peaceful eternity of God – where sorrow, pain and strife are unknown. We collected our rations and the weary Tommies and myself returned to our trenches where we arrived about midnight. Very soon I was in my dugout with dear old Oswald by my side, and before I knew what had happened I was asleep: yes asleep.

Oh! Whilst we were waiting for the rations to come up, I came across a party of Tommies who belonged to the Suffolk regt. We soon commenced a conversation and I found that several came from Sudbury and other familiar districts. It was quite a happy meeting. During our long tramp, when coming to the trenches, we passed through one ville which was in a shocking state. Every house was a total wreck and the lovely old church was blown to atoms. High on one roof a cross could be seen by the light of the moon: I breathed "By this sign thou shalt conquer". Although the church was ruined, the many tombstones appeared to be untouched and the crowded crosses afforded a striking and deep spectacle in the moonlight. We soon passed through those silent streets and were once again in the open, with only the explosions of shells and the cracking of rifles to break the stillness of the night. When the rest came I was soon laid prone upon the stony and rough track, but before I had been many minutes upon my back, the words sounded ADVANCE. Off we tramped and finally we arrived at the trenches tired out.

(NO FINAL PAGE)

Fourteenth Letter

B. Ex. Force, Belgium
23rd Sunday after Trinity
7 November 1915

"For our conversation is in heaven: from whence also we look for the Saviour, the Lord Jesus Christ, who shall change our vile body, that it may be fashioned like unto his glorious body, according to the working whereby he is able even to subdue all things unto himself." Phil. iii v.xx

My dearest parents and all,

The glorious Sabbaths of the Trinity feast are fast rolling away and in a short space of time the ancient feast of Advent will dawn upon this troublesome world. Little did I think last year at this time, that my Advent communion would be made in the ruined plains of brave Belgium. I have just received Mary's kind and treasured letter and so glad to hear of her new appointment in the Record office. I trust, dear girl, that you will like the work and certainly you are doing your bit by releasing a man fit for service. The parcel has not yet come but perhaps tomorrow's mail will favour me, although I must not grumble, as today I have had 6 letters and a lovely parcel from Mrs Richardson of the Mount, York. There is a lovely farm pie inside made of bacon etc and some fine teacakes.

I am delighted to hear that my last Sunday's letter arrived safely and that the ring fits Pater. I was wondering whether the ring would arrive safely as it was so huge. Don't you think it is well made? I must thank ……. You will perhaps wonder why I have not sent a letter during the week. Really I have been so busy with my new job and being in the so-called REST camp every moment of my time has been occupied. This camp is not a rest camp – the same old business - all work and really this period out of the trenches is hardly welcomed.

I see one of the October's John Bull magazines has been commenting on our Div. John Bull says "Who is this mysterious Division who hold the most advanced part of the British Front? Who is this Division who has held the line for 4 months where the Regulars couldn't hold it? Who is this Division who work always and get no rest?. Who are these men who came out 16,000 strong and are now only 7,000 strong? WHO are these men?" So you see we are featured in John Bull, and he in the above words speaks on the work and abilities of our Division. However such does not alter the condition of us and here we are, and here we shall remain until the "Bosche Eagle" is laid low.

" Ils ne passeront pas "
"Old soldiers never say die they'll simply block the way"

The whole camp is under mud and water and conditions are far from comfortable. My boots have been wet through for weeks and have no chance of drying. My feet are nearly always cold except when I am walking about. We are to return to the trenches earlier than expected, so again our REST is cut short by days. However we shan't want to come to this "White Elephant Camp" again.

I am so pleased to hear that Billy and his people came to see you last Sunday. I am glad that he is getting on well – give him my love. I say I do miss Old Oswald but I expect to hear from him shortly and then I shall be relieved.[10]

Now I will answer a few of your questions. Firstly I am still in the West Yorks – I am not in the R.A.M.C. *(Royal Army Medical Corps)*. Neither have I anything to do with that section of the army. Wherever my Batt. goes, I go. I am simply looking after the medical work and equipment. Just like the cooks look after the food etc. I am attached to the Headquarters. staff because it is a staff job. It does not mean that, being attached to H'qrs., I don't go in the trenches etc. Where the men go, I go: So I hope you understand that point. I am still in D. Company. My job is still in the trenches, but a different routine. The danger is just the same and I can assure you all that I shall take all the care of myself as I possibly can. The hardships will be just the same, only instead of blazing away with a rifle, I shall be attending to the sick and wounded, and being with

10 *Oswald was his erstwhile dug-out companion. A letter recording Oswald's transfer/wounding is missing.*

Hqrs. I may get a little extra food occasionally and other comforts. I am forging ahead with my work which appeals to me very strongly. I love the work and already I have seen many wonderful things.[11] Oh, I get plenty of candles now and shall not require any more MILK thanks. I say my feet are like lead and my wet socks won't help to warm them. All the leaves are now fallen from the battered trees and the whole country looks barren and miserable. The frosts don't half bite and the nights are very cold. The rain has made conditions fearful and the whole country is a mud mire. Part of my spare time is spent in studying the necessary points in connection with my new work.

To my great joy I had the opportunity of partaking in the blessed sacrament again this morning. The service was as usual held in a ruined barn and notwithstanding the position, the service was simple but beautiful in all its sacredness. I was sorry so few attended, as really these services are so divine and eagerly awaited. Do you know my dear ones, I felt so near to you this morning during that sweet hour. You almost seemed to be present with me. What a glorious thought the Communion of Saints is, and this awful war has even made this divine blessing more real and sacred. My duties this morning prevented me attending the morning Batt. Service 10.30.

Now a word about the yarn that I had been made Sergt. This is untrue. I still rank as a Corpl. but have taken over full Sergt's duties and I expect, as soon as I master the job and get settled, I shall be awarded the extra stripe. I am as well off as a Sgt., but don't get the pay which however is not much more than my present pay, as I get 1st Class Proficiency Pay for a 1st class shot. The extra stripe is sure to come and I shan't press the matter as I am alright and I know I am doing the work as well as holding the responsibility. So you will now see the position which is TIT for TAT.

I will now probably surprise you a little. This week, all being well, a parcel will arrive which possesses the Xmas presents for you all. The reason for this seeming absurd undertaking I will now explain. This week we return to the trenches for a long, long spell and when we return to REST billets it will be the season de Nöel. By that season all the good articles will have flown, also there is a great risk of the parcel being lost or delayed when the postal pressure is heavy. "Compris"? The parcel will contain the following: "Lace Table centre" for Mother and Pater, all hand-made; Lace collarette for Aunt Pol. with Valencian work (hand made); Lace handkerchiefs for Barbara and Mary with Vlcn. Lace border (hand-made); Brooch like famous 75mm for Flo and Cannon; French 75mm for Edward; a small charm (German Helmet) is for Pater, which I hope he will like. I also send two china saucers which we have rescued from some of the ruins in Ypres. These I hope will arrive safely and will be a splendid souvenir. There will also be 4 crosses. One each for Aunt, Florence, Edith and Madeline. Oh is there anyone else who you think would want a cross?. In the parcel will also be about 3 doz P.C.s, which are a splendid collection showing the ruins of Ypres etc. Do look after them please. No doubt they will interest many friends. In one of the match boxes

---

11 *It seems that doing this medical work, helping with the sick and wounded, which he clearly enjoyed, sowed the seeds which led to him studying Medicine after the war. It is not surprising that his family got the impression he was in the R.A.M.C. He finally qualified as a doctor in 1926.*

will be 3 interesting souvenirs, which please <u>save</u>. A French bullet partly carved, a drummer's badge and a bullet shaped *(draws a diagram here)*. This bullet nearly had the cheek to pot me – as a matter of fact it just missed me and I picked it up as a souvenir on account of its history. I propose sending three of the little crosses to the Vicar's daughters – do you think they would care for them? As soon as the parcel arrives please let me know. The whole of the lace is guaranteed genuine hand made Belgian. Being made within shell fire makes the lace very interesting and it is also very scarce indeed. In fact all the officers are after it like new gold and this makes the price rattle up and also makes the lace scarce.

The war seems to be no nearer the finish but great things may happen before long – at least I hope so. I went to a certain town yesterday and had a royal time – I made a deep hole in my pocket but I enjoyed myself immensely. I had a great meal consisting of Roast Pork, Peas, Potatoes, Coffee etc and the clean plate made the meal so enjoyable. Really it was a treat to have a good meal, well-served. I went with the intention of having a good tuck in even if it cost me a 100 francs. I went to a concert in the evening which was 1st class and the programme was very well rendered.

I might say that I have wrapped my blanket round my feet and they are quite warm. I have been very busy attending to some sick tonight and this has delayed my letter, which I fear will be rather uninteresting. My new job fully occupies my time, so please excuse any neglect in my correspondence. I should like a nice flash light, a reliable one as it will be most useful to me. Get one that will take refills and one that has a strong case. Mr Coverdale would supply me with a good article.

I am glad to hear about your recruiting successes Pater dear – you seem to be very busy. Have you started the real hunting yet – you will be able to scrape in two days a week won't you? I suppose the garden is looking very shabby now – you must have had a wonderful fruit crop. I feel sure the wounded will feel very grateful to you for your frequent consignments. There is a little ring for one of you in the parcel. How do you like your ring Barbie dear? I was charmed with your lovely letter which was beautifully written. You do write lovely letters. I was delighted with your letter dear Aunt also.

Well how are you all at dear old home? I wonder when I shall see it again. I feel sure that God will grant me this rich blessing; something tells me that before long I shall see your dear faces. May heaven grant this. Mother darling how are you? I pray that you are happy and well – I long to feel your dear lips pressing with that perfect love against my face. Your dear voices will seem so strange – but yet I often seem to hear them. God will answer your prayers in his own good time, so put your whole trust in him. The wait may be long but heavenly comfort will be granted unto you.

I must prepare a close, as the candle is nearly burnt out and it is getting very late. I would like a complete Bible very much – you can get an Active Service edition which is thin and has a canvas cover to protect it. Poor Mary …….. I am very well and enjoying the best of health, which is a great blessing.

My fondest love and kisses to you all my dearest ones. I will conclude by committing you all unto the divine protection of our dear Lord. May his mighty arm ever guard you from all harm and evil. …….. May God guide me again to my Father's house in peace – MIZPAH. Good-night xx.

Believe me.
Ever your loving Son,
Arthur G Wilson Cpl.
B.E.F.
XXXXXXXX

Shortly after writing this letter, my father was awarded his commission and returned to "Blighty" for training and a happy reunion with his family.

Two elements loom large in Peter's letters home. His parcels and the vehemence of the artillery barrages.

The most popular man in the regiment.
The smiling military postman with the mail from "Blighty".

This mountain of empty shell cases gives a vivid idea of the scale of the
artillery barrages.

Episode Two
Subaltern Peter Wilson Rejoins His Regiment

My father, having completed his training, returned to his regiment in France, as a 2nd Lieutenant, in July 1916. At this time the 1/5th West Yorks were on the Somme in front of Albert, holding a section of the front near Thiepval. Only one letter survives from this period. Peter's memoirs serve to bring alive more details of life for a young officer at the front in 1916. Allow me to quote:

Back Among Friends:

"My batman and I joined the returning troops and marched with them to join the Battalion, who were holding a section of the line in Thiepval Wood. After a long march, with intermittent rest for the fatigue party to ease their weary shoulders, we finally arrived at the reserve line of trenches. I reported to the Adjutant at Battalion Headquarters situated in a deep dugout. I knew him during my 1914/15 spell with the Regiment and he gave me a great welcome. It was another pleasant surprise when I met my old Colonel, who had been C/O of the 5th Battalion West Yorkshire Regiment since August 4th 1914, when the Battalion mobilised. Quite a wonderful feeling came over me when I realised that I was back once again with my old Regiment and with so many of my old comrades. A guide led me through a maze of deep communications trenches and we finally arrived at D Company Headquarters which were in a dugout and consisted of four wire-supported wooden bunks, two wooden stools and a small wooden table, where four could eat a meal. Two of my brother Officers were asleep in the dugout, which had two candles as the only means of illumination, and one Subaltern was out on duty visiting front line trench positions."

Snipers – A deadly hazard:

"The German sniper, using a rifle fitted with a telescopic sight, was a deadly shot and often used a shell torn tree or partly destroyed building to take up a firing position which had a clear view of a short area of the British front line trench. He never used the same firing point twice and, as his carefully camouflaged position was almost ten to twelve feet above ground level, he was able to get a clear view of the British trench and obtain a view of the head and shoulders of the troops. I had the tragic experience of seeing three of my comrades who were quite close to me, fall victim to a deadly shot and they were killed instantly. It was impossible to tell from which direction the shot was fired, as during "Stand to" there was usually an uninterrupted inferno from shell fire and bursts of machine gun and rifle fire. I was once in a prepared Sniper Post which was protected by a special iron plate with a loop-hole, which allowed my rifle to protrude and allow me to align my sights on an enemy target 150 yards away in enemy front line trenches. I was in the firing position and lying prone with my rifle butt adjacent to my right shoulder when, quite suddenly there was a metallic bang, and

an enemy sniper's bullet had actually entered through the small hole in the metal plate and struck the back sight of my rifle. How it missed hitting me I do not know, but I must admit I was greatly shocked and promptly moved the protecting iron plate to a totally different angle. This demonstrates the incredible accuracy of the enemy sniper."

And later: A Courageous Signaller:

"The power of the enemy gunfire was so intense on our forward area that most of the overhead telephone wires were totally destroyed and it was impossible to make contact with Headquarters for urgent messages. Notwithstanding the havoc caused by the shell fire, the bravery and determination of the company signallers was incredible, as they struggled to restore the destroyed lines of communication."

"THROUGH"

This sketch shows a gallant Signaller who goes out specially to mend the all-important telephone cable which has been cut by shell fire. After a long search for the broken line, he finally discovers the "break" and under heavy shell fire mends the cable. With his "tapping in" wire he joyfully establishes communication with his unit, and the Troops in the advanced post are again in direct contact with the artillery behind. Suddenly, a screech tears the desolated village and shrapnel finds its mark. Stricken in death he falls (his work completed as he is "THROUGH" to his Headquarters) and as his vision fades, he gazes towards the little Crucifix with outstretched arms. Then "all" is peace.

The little Grotto even helps to support the German barbed wire – a reminder of the "Crown of Thorns", emblems of the first Calvary.

No mother or sweetheart will ever know how her dear one met his end – they merely heard from the War Office "Regret to report your son Signaller ?? No. 02743 is "missing", believed killed."

> *No medal hangs from his brave chest*
> *But poppies bloom and in the trees, birds sing*
> *His gallant spirit claimed by God doth rest*
> *And as the sunset fades each day, bells ring.*

This sketch and verse is dedicated to the memory of a gallant "West Yorks Signaller" who fell 3 September 1916 Thiepval. The sketch was drawn by Peter after the incident which much moved him.

A Narrow Shave:

We always seemed to have heavy days of action on Sundays. On one Sunday in early September the heavy artillery barrage raged all day and casualties were heavy. Darkness had fallen and I was having a short rest when my batman said, "A message, sir, for you to report to Battalion Headquarters."

Reporting to the Colonel soon revealed the urgency of his message. "Wilson, the Brigadier is anxious to obtain a German Prisoner and you will be required to conduct a raid into the enemy lines before Thiepval – you will take a raiding party of a Sergeant and 14 men and the artillery will put down a barrage to give you early protection."

After this long hectic day this was a profound surprise and great shock to me, and of course quite a new episode in my young military life. I wondered if I should write a short letter to my parents. I quickly interviewed my Sergeant and the 14 troops and had time for a short meal and hot drink. Bradbury, my batman, fixed me up with my loaded revolver and the raiding party prepared to assemble at the allotted point in the trenches. A quick survey revealed that the Hun had a most formidable line of barbed wire entanglement (Hun wire is very thick and strong). I had some final words with my Colonel and Headquarters Staff and then moved off down the trench towards the sap head, less than 100 yards from German trenches.

It was amazing what thoughts flashed through my mind during these waiting minutes – a prelude to the promised bombardment by our artillery. My raiding party was almost at the point of our sap head, when suddenly up dashed a "Runner" in the narrow trench from Battalion Headquarters. "The Adjutant is on the way to see you, Sir." But before I had time to take in the message, the Adjutant arrived quite breathless. It was only a quarter of an hour before "zero hour". "Wilson," he speedily gave me his message,

"The raid has been cancelled." This message staggered me and through all the Verey lights and shell explosions my eyes penetrated the canopy of gloom and smoke, and all the stars seemed to encompass me with their celestial glory.

I quickly told my Raiding Party and we seemed to be walking on air as we wended our way back through the maze of narrow trenches to Battalion Headquarters.

A West Yorks raiding party (War Illustrated March 1916)

Fifteenth Letter

12th Sunday after Trinity
B.E.F.
10 Sep. 16

"Teach me to do the thing that pleaseth thee, for Thou art my God: let Thy loving spirit lead me forth into the land of righteousness. Psalms. CXLiii v.x

My dearest Parents,

I was delighted to receive your welcome letter yesterday, which was written last Sunday, as I had been anxiously waiting for a letter from home for several days. I can't understand why dear Barbara's lovely letters, for the last two Sundays, have not yet arrived. The circumstances this Sunday are very different from those of last Sunday. Last Sunday at this time the great stunt[12] was in full swing and raging with intense fury. This Sunday I am resting in a nice little French orchard with only the booming guns to disturb me. How pleasant the change is and I feel heaps of times better for the rest, which was much needed. I expect by the time you receive this letter that I shall be back again in the same part of the line.

I fully expected to hear that Murville would give you a weekend, and I am so pleased he is so fit – I shall look out for him when he comes to this land of strife.

I very much enjoyed reading the Telegraph. The work of the Airman was splendid and he well deserved his V.C. Oh, they want officers to volunteer for the Royal Flying Corps. Would you care for me to submit my name, as I know signalling and Map reading etc.? I am also under the weight limit. Please let me know and it is just as you wish.

I hope my registered parcel arrived yesterday. I regret to say that some of my kit was lost during the stunt last week, including my map case. I hope the map case will turn up. The authorities are doing their best to recover it. Holdick lost the whole of his kit, which was buried with a shell. I have not heard whether Baines has arrived in England or not.

To my great joy I received my first communion since my return to France this morning. Saxby came with me and the divine service was held in a little upper room of a partly destroyed house. Mr Whincup took the service and he was very pleased to see me. I thought of you dear ones at home in our little Parish Church and knew that you would be partaking of the sacred emblems. During the service the roar of the guns was very strong and the countless transports passing on the stony road outside made it very hard for me to hear all the beautiful prayers. But how thankful I was once again to take part

12 Stunt: an intense battle I think.

in the service after those many long and tiring days in the trenches.

Yesterday I had another glorious ride through the long cornfields and my steed was very fit. He simply loved to canter over the soft earth and he enjoyed the fun as much as I did. There are no hedges here at all, so it is possible to canter for hours with only a few ditches to trouble you. The evening was perfect and I went to see an old 5th officer, who was in the R.F.C. at an aerodrome. The steed came home at a great pace and it was glorious to sit in the saddle and canter across acres of land with no one to trouble me. I was in great form when I had dinner and the shaking up did me a lot of good. Oh could you please send me a set of spurs, as I do quite a lot of duty mounted, which needless to say I greatly enjoy.

Although it is Sunday afternoon I am just going on parade and I will finish my letter when parades are over. EXIT.

Parades are now over for the day, so I will endeavour to supply you with the remainder of the news. Last night I went to the second house of the TYKES[13] (who are men who have been selected from our Div.). They gave an excellent show and during the whole of the show the guns were simply roaring like fun. And when we sang *The KING* at the close the volume was tremendous, but even above the strains the guns could be easily heard. Quite a thrill went through me as I sung the grand words as it sounded so wonderful. In fact many of the guns were very near so you could imagine the noise was great. I am very busy training my scouts. My Corporal, a Knaresborough fellow, was wounded last week.

I wonder why the grapes in the hothouse are not a success? Has the root been watered and fed??? We can get plenty of pears and apples here and they are very cheap so I should not send any in parcels. Besides fruit soon crushes and then the whole parcel is ruined. I tell you what would be nice, a roasted chicken sent out and well covered with fat. Please don't forget my Allum Block (Chrystaline Block) which I use after shaving, also a shaving stick. The flower buds must look lovely now and the Worcester Pearmain[14] will soon be ready for the table. Many thanks for the statement of my Pass Book. I see that Sept. pay and July allowances are not yet credited.

Have you had a day out cubbing yet? I suppose many packs have bowled over many Cubs. You must keep the ball rolling; if it stops it will never roll again!! Eddie seems to be enjoying himself at Newport and I suppose Cyril will visit you shortly. My fly net is "hors de combat", so please send me another (brown or green). Send a net, not silk as it is hard to breathe through. Make it in the shape of a bag then it will fall over my head. The other way it falls off when I sleep and the Mosquito does his work.

I am glad Aunt and Flop enjoyed their holiday in Wales. I will write to Aunt this week. The country here looks so pretty with the acres and acres of crops all in stooks. The

---

13 A concert party.
14 A pear.

people make such funny shaped stooks. They make the stook and then put a sheaf on top upside down and so the rain runs off. Rather a good idea.
(Here there was a diagram of a hay stook.)

I enjoyed my visit to Amiens very much and the Lobster was lovely! The cathedral is really very fine and the shops also very good.

This letter is very uninteresting because I am unable to give you any war news due to the censors, so you see one has very little to write about.

Well my dearest ones I hope you are all well and happy. I am expecting a letter, Mother darling, today so I hope the mail arrives.

May God grant you all his peace and many blessings.

My fondest love and xx^s to you all. Goodbye for the present, I must have told you all the news. My very best wishes to all my dear friends in Haxby. MIZPAH.

Ever your loving son,
Arthur G Wilson

P.S. The Cake and Raisins etc were ripping.

EXTRACT OF 1973 LETTER

Home, Radlett

15 IX 73

My Dearest All,

As I write this date, as above, I am reminded of 57 years ago, when, right at the height of the Battle of the Somme, I sat on my charger (as ordered by my Colonel) and watched "The Tanks" go into action for the <u>FIRST</u> time. What a thrill and I was only 1 mile from the front line - the roar of battle was tremendous and screaming shells were flying overhead – I was indeed lucky to find my way back to my Regimental Headquarters and make my report – Incidentally I think I was the only mounted officer in that sector of the line that day. The next week, in the same sector, I had an argument with a high explosive shell which put me out of action for a year.

Quite a contrast today "Battle of Britain" Saturday. I have been on duty at the R.A.F. Jumble Stall in the village and did a roaring trade with the book stall – fine weather brought out the public and we ended up with £74 – highly successful. The Jumble stall was like Petticoat Lane and the "JUNK" sold like hot cakes!!!! ….

To give you a better idea of conditions faced by our soldiers, I am including some photographs and war artists' impressions.

"A British Tank"

A typical trench. "New Zealanders south of the Ancre, September 1916."

I am indebted to the War Illustrated, dated 9th September 1916, for this graphic illustration:

"THE CAMPBELLS ARE COMING!" - The first rush of the Highland regiments for Longueval was one of the finest exploits of the war. Their pipers led them right across the German lines, one regiment advancing to the tune "The Campbells are Coming!". Then the pipes screamed out the "Charge!" and with fixed bayonets and hand-grenades the Highlanders stormed the German trenches. When all was over, the pipers led the Highlanders back from the trenches, playing an old Scottish love-melody.

Disaster

Two weeks after writing the previous letter, on September 23rd 1916, my father was very severely wounded when manning a solitary observation post in "No Man's Land". For four days he had been sending back maps and drawings of the German lines, into which he could easily see. A shell landed right on top of his concealed outpost. He was very severely wounded in both thighs and elsewhere. Indeed, he carried a couple of unextractable shell splinters in his thighs all his life.

Allow me to share his description of this event, which occurred only 10 weeks after he rejoined his regiment as a young officer. Young Subaltern's life expectancy was very short indeed.

"The Colonel sent for me and said how sorry he was to cut short my rest. I would have to leave that very night to make a special visit to the front line forward observation post "Jacob's Ladder", which was at Beaumont Hamel. This post was unique as from its well-concealed position, it had a clear view of the German trench system at Thiepval and "The Triangle" adjacent to the Schwaben Redoubt, just the other side of the River Ancre. It was a long heavy tramp and I had Bradbury to care for my comforts. I slept on the floor of this small Ob. Post.

"I was very early on duty and from my small concealed peep hole I could see right into the German trenches and the massive Schwaben Redoubt. I had a complete close-up view with my telescope, and made observations on a special map on which I located strong concrete machine gun positions along the whole German Front Line. It was exciting to get close up views of the German soldiers in their trenches and fortified strong points. I had been provided with an up to date trench map, with all German trench systems printed in red. I was able to plot several dozen machine gun points, even back to the German Reserve line. After two days' intense and non-stop observations I made a detailed map, with all the vital posts and trench strong points carefully recorded. These were taken by special courier back to Brigade Headquarters. These vital details were to assist the preparation for the coming big attack in a few days time. The companies carrying out the first wave of attack were provided with information on all the enemy concrete machine guns posts and the heavily protected barbed wire zones. I continued to make further inspections during my third and fourth days in Jacob's ladder and was able to dispatch my second detailed report to Brigade Headquarters on the Saturday afternoon.

23rd September 1916

"As dusk fell on my fourth night in Jacob's ladder, I had just settled for the night, after my batman had provided me with a meal and hot drink. I stretched out on the floor of this small O.Post, which had a protected roof and supported sides. Heavy shelling was going on and one could see the whole line of the battle front, north and south, by the Verey light spectacle and the hundreds of exploding shells.

"I was soon asleep, when without any warning there was a sudden tremendous crash and mighty explosion, as the whole O.P. structure crashed in upon me and buried me in a mass of heavy material. A mighty eight-inch shell had made a direct hit on the OP and the rank smell of cordite added to the grim tragedy. The heavy explosion had knocked me clean out and I could not feel my legs, or move my arms, with the weight of material debris over me. I could only breathe with difficulty. Eventually I heard voices and Bradbury was the first to make contact with me."

With great courage, his loyal batman, BRADBURY, and a stretcher party managed to rescue him from the shattered remains of his hidden observation post in "No Man's Land". He was losing a lot of blood, especially from the wounds in his thighs. He was gently carried to the nearest advanced dressing station where his eighteen (he thought) wounds were cleaned and dressed, and he received anti-tetanus and morphine injections. His stretcher was then placed under a hedge, alongside many other casualties, for the remainder of the night. He remembered being woken by an anxious Bradbury with a cup of tea, and later a little French girl presenting him with a posy of flowers.

He spent some time in hospitals in France before being evacuated to England where he was to spend another 3 months in Leicester Military Hospital, followed by a further three months convalescence. After that he was given light duties before being passed fit for overseas duties.

Three days after these events, British troops captured the trenches Peter had been spying on.

Sadly, the faithful Bradbury did not survive the war. The Commonwealth War Graves Commission informs me that he was killed on November 20th, 1917, and is buried in Favreuil British Cemetery.

Episode Three
Back to France for the third time

In July 1917, Peter's wounds were sufficiently healed for him to return to his beloved West Yorks Regiment in France.

Extracts from diary:

28ᵗʰ July 1917
It was amazing how hard all the troops worked on the wiring and on the trench building, as the Battalion were holding an advanced "region" which had only recently been captured from the Germans in the Battle of Bullecourt. By the time the Battalion went out of the trenches for a week we had constructed a splendid strong belt of barbed wire defences.

These two extracts from his memoirs give a graphic description of patrols in "No Man's Land".

<u>With 3/5 W Yorks near Bullecourt.</u>
"*I tried to sleep on wire bed – wounds v. painful and I could not lie on either side. Had to see Battalion M.O. as wounds not properly healed – all right in proper bed with mattress and sheets. All this first week went on wiring parties for all the hours of darkness.*

"*On 4ᵗʰ night ordered to take control of large patrol in "No Man's Land". Sergt. and 14 men. Went on long 12 to 3 a.m. reconnonaissance into No Man's Land. Very dark night and Verey lights often gave no help. V. slow silent progress and we did not bump into enemy patrol. I lost my revolver when crawling and had to make a diligent search in the dark. After long search actually placed my hand on the barrel of the revolver.*"

And again:
"*No Man's Land is very vague and we made a great long trek into the unknown and finally returned to our own zone of No Man's Land at 3 a.m. But here let me tell you of an exciting episode when out in No Man's Land. My Sergt. approached me, having mustered the full patrol about half a mile from our trench system. He said, "We must return this way, Sir," and to my surprise the patrol was facing due EAST – direct to the German lines. This night was clear, with all the celestial star system showing bright. I had studied the stars for several years and there to the S.E. was my favourite constellation " ORION" in all his glory. I told the Sergt. "Do sit down and listen to me", I said firmly. "If you go the way you suggest you will all be shot or taken prisoner before dawn." I pointed out Orion to him and said "That position is S.E. and leads straight to the German lines." He didn't trust my decision – "We must go in exactly the opposite direction," I ordered. We then mustered the patrol and slowly made our way back. After half an hour we found ourselves challenged by a Scots sentry. We were only three hundred yards from the West Yorkshire trenches. Dawn was*

breaking when we reached our own zone and all eager for that early cup of tea. We had been on patrol for four hours in No Man's Land and now had to face half an hour of "Stand to" and wait until full sunlight had taken control. My Sergt. came up to me and apologised for his stubbornness about the route for the return to our own lines. He appeared grateful for the way I explained the crisis to him."

Sixteenth Letter

NOTE: The next surviving letter was written after his return to France in 1917. In fact his extensive wounds were not sufficiently healed for trench warfare. He applied to join the R.F.C. and while waiting to know if his application was successful, he was sent on an advanced signals course in a chateau at Pas-en-Artois. This letter must have been written just after his arrival for the course.

11th Sunday After Trinity
19 8 17
B.E.F.

My dearest Parents,

I have just arrived at the highest point of the Forest and I am sitting in a lovely glade which overlooks a charming vale below – Stretched out in front are long stretches of cornfields, most of which are now in stooks. It is a glorious day and a lovely breeze is blowing. The absence of hedges reminds me of colonial views and the rolling vale is dotted with transport lines etc. Well, my dearest ones, I s'pose you are now again quite used to home life after the holidays. I hope you are both better after the change.

This morning I went to the Church in the town and saw the whole of the service through. Of course the service was all in French, but nevertheless the service was very nice. The Sunday School children were rather well behaved, although an old gentleman, dressed up like Napoleon, wearing a three cornered hat, had to rebuke them with a long gilt pole at intervals. We had 3 collections and the acolytes were ringing bells during the whole of the service. Everyone partakes in the Mass even the children.

I was very charmed to receive all the letters last Thursday and dear Barbie's on Friday. I have got a large pile of apples, pears and chocolates here, so I am well equipped for the afternoon. I shall not return for tea but get back in time for dinner. There are 3 of us here and the continual chattering does not allow me to concentrate my mind.

I have had a stiff time during the last week and you can well imagine how I enjoy the rest. Last night I had a great time – really the best since I have been in France. I had an invitation to spend the evening with the Notary of the town – about 4 of us went. We had quite a jolly evening. I sang four songs and about half- a-dozen ladies (French) jabbered in French and occasionally in English. I almost forgot that a war was on –

An officer, a lovely player, rendered Rachmanninoff, Beethoven and Greig and other lovely music. One of the girls sang in French *"Softly wakes my heart"* and other good items. About 12 of us were in the room and the noise was remarkable – I attempted to speak French with little success and it was most amusing when we tried to explain various things. The Notary is a dear old gentleman and most hospitable. Finally, after shaking hands for 20 minutes, we departed just after 11.

After coming out, we officers went for a lovely walk in the moonlight and watched the flashes of the guns. At present the guns are very busy near here and very angry at nights. Now do you like the photos of P.; don't you think the town very pretty, also the Castle?? At present I am writing from one of the places shown.

We had a celebration at the Chateau this morning, also a short form of matins. Both services were so welcome. Our Adjutant Is the Earl of Malmesbury (the 5th Earl) I believe he is an Irish peer – do you know the family??

I am glad the first parcel of souvenirs has arrived. I hope the 'Helmet' and 'Tank' souvenirs have arrived now, also your parcel Mother darling. Our mails are very erratic here and we only get them every few days. I hope dear Auntie and Uncle are enjoying their visit to the parish. I hope they are both well. There are simply stones of lovely brambles here and they are wasting. I have eaten so many that my tongue is quite purple. These boys are chattering so much that I cannot possibly write any longer.

Well my dearest ones I have really told you all the news of interest so I will now close – Excuse the scrawl as my knee is my writing desk.

I hope you are all well – and I trust your sciatica is better Pater dear, also your heels Mother darling. I really must close now so send my fondest love and xxs to you all.

My best love to dear Uncle and Auntie as ever.

Dominus Vobis cum
Ever your loving Son,
A G W.
Xxxx

p.s. Excuse any mistakes as I have been interrupted throughout this letter.
I have just sketched a panoramic view which I get from the top of the Hill.

(No diagram.)

Just got back and going in to dinner.

Episode Four
With The Royal Flying Corps
(November 1917 – December 1919)

Less than two months after being accepted for the R.F.C., on September 18th, 1917, my father returned to France as a fully qualified R.F.C. Observer with the rank of Lieutenant. He joined 7 Squadron based near Proven in November.

Only two letters have survived from his time with the R.F.C., so I think a few extracts from his diaries about this hair-raising period of his life will serve to give readers a more comprehensive image of Peter's experiences in France.

11th November 1917
"Instructions from Air Ministry to report to 2nd Wing RFC Boulogne. Left Victoria 7.35 and had comfortable crossing to Boulogne. On arrival at 42 Sqdn., there is much excitement as the Sqdn. has orders to proceed to Italy on the morrow. When having interview with Adjutant urgent message comes through from 2nd wing to say No. 7 Sqdn at Proven near Poperinge has lost several machines and aircrew and needs replacement observers. Adjt. asks me if I would not mind being posted to No. 7 Sqdn. – I willingly agree.

14th November 1917
"Report at Sqdn Office to meet C.O. Maj. B E Sutton DSO MC, of the Cumberland Yeomanry. Posted to the "Contact Flight B" and Johnson-Gilbert to be my Pilot. A dull day, unfit for flying, so a party is organised for Poperinge with Facey[15] and Durham. Tea at La Poupee where we meet "Ginger", who appears to be on most affectionate terms with Durham. Suppose she is with most of the B.E.F.!

Go with Gilly to Stores to collect my Flying Kit and maps. Then examine B Flight Hangar and our RE8 Machine. I make thorough examination of my "rear" seat position, examine M.G. (machine gun) mounting and wireless details and camera installations.

21st November 1917
"Flying again – repeat photos 500 feet over Salient and take low flying views of trenches. Hun machine guns pepper our machine but no serious damage. After flight I take machine gun practice on rifle range. Orderly Officer today, have good opportunity of seeing men and their huts. Men have comfortable beds and good food.

---

15 Rex Facey became a doctor and also a life long friend.

After more than three years with the West Yorkshire Regiment, an older looking Peter reports for duty in the Royal Flying Corps.

This aerial photograph from Peter's collection gives some idea of the devastation of the French or Belgium countryside, craters everywhere, filled with water, and all houses ruined.

24th November 1917

"Another 'vertical photos' expedition well over "Hun Land" at 8,000 feet. We have excellent Scout Escort of 29 Sqdn. Abundant Archie[16] but we complete our mission and photograph enemy counter battery area."

28th November 1917

"First shoot with Royal Artillery, up 3½ hours with Gilly. In wireless contact with 6" battery – great excitement. Use my wireless to the full and control fire of battery on enemy target. Finally achieve gun battery fire onto large enemy position. Take vertical photos before the shoot and after final battery fire – most successful – we totally destroy enemy target."

30th November 1917

"St Andrew's Day. CO celebrates by inviting Cumberland Yeomanry to dinner. The full band arrive and a Mark I[17] is declared. Many of the Yeomanry pass out early, owing to the potency of No 7 Sqdn's celebration "camouflage" drink mixture. Followed by Stiffman and blind boxing. Now "Stiffman" is played by members sitting on the floor in large circle, feet just far enough apart to permit one man to stand in the centre. This man, holding himself perfectly rigid, falls backwards on to extended arms of one of the "sitters" and is then hurled round at an alarming rate until somebody collapses under the strain. Stiff man and collapsed man exchange places. I have bout of blindfold boxing with Durham, an Australian. I get a very thorough plastering, but only one black eye."

They had a number of parties, but one must remember casualties were very heavy and German planes at times superior. The RFC solution was to make merry rather than mope, and "esprit de corps" was certainly very high.

28th December 1917

"Now extremely cold – my nose frostbitten. Up on Photos. Scout escort most successful. We go far East over Roulers and see Huns in tram cars. Up again in afternoon. Horrocks and Booth in crash. I see impact on aerodrome – looked slight, but Booth incurred fatal head injuries and died in hospital."

That evening, at a time when casualties were very heavy, Peter wrote the following letter in case he was killed. Happily it never had to be sent. He had just turned twenty-three.

---

16 "Archie" was anti-aircraft fire.
17 Mark 1 is a special party. Jolly Pierre must have been in his element among the cheerful lads of the R.F.C. – a stark contrast to the drudgery of trench warfare.

The Seventeenth Letter
The Unsent Letter ......

It was Common practice to write and carry a 'Last Letter' to be sent to loved ones incase of death.
The letter below is Peter's first, written in May 1915.

No. 7 Squadron,
R.F.C., B.E.F.
December 28th 1917

"Be merciful unto me O God, be merciful unto me, for my soul trusteth in Thee, and under the shadow of Thy wings shall be my refuge, make this tyranny be over-past. Psalms LVii v.1

My dearest beloved Father and Mother and all my dear ones at home,

I now write you a final letter, which I trust will be a great comfort to you all, if it be the divine will of my dear Lord to call me to my eternal rest during this terrible War.

You all know that throughout this fearful conflict my whole trust has been cast upon my precious Saviour. Through all these long and critical periods the unseen presence has been so near to me – an unspeakable comfort, a treasured and constant companion. I often thank my gracious Lord for his great blessings, which he bestowed upon me by granting me safe returns to you all on several occasions during this war. What a glorious thing Prayer is – a sacred communion with the Almighty. I know how earnest your prayers are when, before retiring every night, you all join together in that beautiful Family Prayer which is so perfect in God's sight. What a blessing was bestowed upon us all last Easter, when the whole family knelt before the Altar of our dear little Parish Church. That surely was an answer to Prayer. May God grant that as a family we may worship together in the celestial courts above.

It is hard to find words in order to express my thanks for all your unceasing kindness to me during these long months. I often thank my loving Father for the blessed home he has given to me. My prayer is "May He grant me a safe return to my Home in peace". God be praised for blessing me with such Christlike parents and my dear loving Sisters and Brother. My dearest Father and Mother, how precious you are to me and may the Almighty shower down upon you his richest blessings for many years to come. Your tender words to me have always been carefully registered in my heart and have helped me to live a straight life.

Barbara and Mary my dearest Sisters, how sweet and devoted you have been to me. I know what comfort and joy you have given to dearest Father and Mother. Your labours for the Master will surely receive a reward. Continue to serve Him and true happiness and joy will always be yours. Edward my dear brother, I pray that you put your whole trust in God. He will guide you in the path of the righteous – the path of life is no easy task – to live a clean, straight life is very hard – I feel sure you will fulfil pure and holy ideals and prove a joy and comfort to my dearest ones.

If it be the will of my dear Lord to call me to his Holy presence, may you find comfort in knowing that I possess a joyful heart, knowing that I have done my best to fight the battle of life. I feel so happy and I possess a deep spirit of peace – I simply cling to the Cross and whatsoever He wills – must be. If I make the journey beyond – to that brighter home – I pray that He will grant you His Holy spirit and help you to bear the sorrow. Such spiritual comfort is far above any which this world can afford.

I am indeed proud to think that I am here doing my bit for my dear old Country, my King and my beloved home. It is a glorious thing to fight for one's country and in a cause for freedom. May God grant us victory, which will lead to a glorious peace and to the further extension of his Kingdom on Earth. What a happy day for all – when the world will utter forth the thanksgivings of a just and righteous peace. I hope and pray that that glorious day is not far distant, may it be soon.

It is time to conclude, so my dearest ones I will say farewell in Christ Jesus. I pray that as a family we may be reunited in the realms above. If I meet you not again on earth I shall wait in glory at the golden gates of Eternity. There, beside my dear Lord, you will be welcomed by the Prince of Peace and together we shall enter that House of many mansions, where for ever as a family we shall fall down and worship before the Throne of God and the Lamb. May these words welcome you as you enter the realms of eternity, "Well done good and faithful servants enter thou into the joys of my Lord". What a day of rejoicing when all loved ones will be reunited – thus transplanted to rise and shine in Heaven. May Heaven's richest blessings be showered down upon you all and may happiness and joy ever reign within the walls of our dear home. My dearest love to you all, my dearest ones. Do not lament – but say "It is Thy will O Lord". Remember some day we shall meet again and nothing can then separate us – we shall be for ever with the Lord.

My dearest Father and Mother good bye, my dearest Barbara and Mary and Edward farewell – Mother darling cheer up the home – dearest Father will be a great source of comfort. I will close thanking and praising God for His many and rich blessings which he has abundantly bestowed upon me. I shall always go into action trusting wholly in my Creator. He will cover my head in the day of battle. I am so happy and I do not fear the battle – my dear Lord is waiting for me – if he calls me to his eternal presence, I breathe "O Lamb of God I come".

"Finally, dear ones farewell, be perfect, be of good comfort, be of one mind. Live in peace and the God of love and peace shall be with you". I commit you all unto the divine keeping of God, may His manifold blessings be showered down upon you and may the Holy Spirit of God strengthen you.

My dearest love to you all – Farewell in Christ Jesus.

I remain,
Ever your beloved Son,
Arthur G Wilson
Lt. R.F.C.

A photograph of 7 Squadron, with Squadron Leader Bertie Sutton in the centre of the second row, and Peter fourth from left in front row. Note the huge variety of uniforms indicating that the R.F.C. drew its aircrew from many regiments, Bertie Sutton from the Cumberland Yeomanry sounded highly suitable for an airman! Some look incredibly young.

The Diary Continues

19th January 1918
First round of Wing Rugger Cup on Aerodrome – match played against No 9 Sqdn. Immense gathering including the Chinese. We play at top of our form, especially Isett and John Vic. Borman opens scoring with drop goal. Wilmott and I score tries with both conversions by Peter Holm. Half time 14 pts to 0. Second half still on top of our form. Gilly presents me with 2 more tries, one conversion – then Firth scores after long run. We win 1 drop goal, 3 goals, 3 tries to 1 try, 28 pts. to 3. A Mark I celebration declared and the Binge Boys[18] celebrate – a tremendous night – very few in for breakfast. The two horses arrive, one a large grey.

21st January 1918
Went for a ride – mounted the grey – disgraceful scene as horse bolts and makes for Proven. Notice on board "Horses must go through village at the walk." Belgian Police attempt to stop me – horse gallops through village on cobblestones, jumps clean over motor bike and side-car and finally halted at the big level crossing gates. I take horse through flooded area to tire him out. Finally return quietly to Sqdn. and have my leg severely pulled. I find the horse is blind in one eye!

23rd January 1918
Up with Gilly over Allsopp's Farm, exciting 10 minutes with Hun machine-gun duel. Machine hit and left tail control shot away. Great difficulty in flying back, I wireless for ambulance to stand by. Gilly does very well, but we crash heavily on landing. We didn't catch fire and I am sawn out of wreckage after half an hour – luckily both escape serious injury, apart from local bruising. We are sent up immediately on another 3 hour patrol and return aching. C.O. and Flight Commanders gazing on wreckage.

When on aerodrome we suddenly see an observer falling from a 9 Squadron machine. He falls 300 feet and is killed.
(Note: I don't suppose their safety belts were very strong, if indeed they existed at all. And in those early days the airmen had no parachutes.)

12th – 26th February 1918
Leave.

Grand to be home again with the family. My brother, Edward, gets leave at same time from his ship. Have an excellent day's hunting with the York and Ainsty Foxhounds – given an excellent mount – young four year old hunter, very fresh – plenty of Military

---

18 The young men of 7 Squadron were quite something! Bertie Sutton stayed on in the RAF and became a much respected Air Marshall and was knighted; Leonard Isett became Air Vice Marshall Sir Leonard Isett, Chief of New Zealand Air Staff; Maurice Harland became Bishop of Durham 1955-1966; Ian Johnson-Gilbert, "Gilly", became Sir Ian Johnson-Gilbert and was Lord Provost of Edinburgh, among other things. They all became friends for life.

out and we have superb run over grass. Meet at famous Askham Bogs and soon find fox and then pack run over the cream of the Y and A country. I take a toss at one big hedge and my Father says, "Come and take my mount, that young horse is too much for you." So I change my mount and ride his aged hunter. One Senior Officer who saw my embarrassment says, "Young Man, I think flying suits you better than hunting!" However, I join in the hunt again and have a super ride on my father's mount. We have a long ride home together after a most enjoyable day's hunting.

4th March 1918 – Rugger Final against No. 21 Sqdn.
Huge crowd and all No 9 Sqdn turn up to support us. They fire lots of Verey lights and noise from klaxon horns tremendous. The game commenced at a tremendous rate and No 21 nearly score.

Our forwards then take control, Isett breaks away supported by John Vic (H.A.C.). Isett sells a perfect dummy and scores a super try. Peter Wilson (himself) converts goal. Klaxon horns then deafening.

Then Geoff Borman (South African) scores a second try which I failed to convert. Gilbert superb in tackling and saves certain try. Ding dong struggle most of second half, then just on time, Lane makes a long run down line to score in the corner.

Our forwards splendid and although much lighter than 21 Sqdn, we get most of the ball. The whistle goes for time and W/Cdr Barratt presents the cup.

26th March 1918
Up on early reconnaissance with Maurice Harland, who was at St Peter's School, York, with me. We get lost in terrific ball of cloud and come out well over Hun lines, over Straden. We are heavily archied and I am very windy, as I am only in pyjamas under Flying Kit. Keep a sharp look out for Hun Scouts and I tell Maurice to fly W back into cloud and make for the Belgian area, via the Houlthurst Forest. Most exciting trip, we fly back at 1000 ft and I soon spot Ostende and coastal towns. Then cross Belgian zone and head for Yser canal and our own zone. Finally we find our way to our aerodrome at Proven.

Eighteenth Letter

This letter was written in a period of hectic activity during a major German attack when the RFC were in action constantly, trying to establish the exact location of the front. His squadron were required to be on patrol from dawn to dusk.

"No. 62"
Flanders
8th April 1918

My Dearest Parents,

I expect this letter will arrive one day late in the parish, but I couldn't possibly get a letter off last night. I did not get down from the final patrol of the day until quite late and it was dark before I had dinner. I was also very tired, so I retired immediately after dinner – I thought of you all in the dear little parish church during the hour of evensong and I was doing something so different. I had the joy of attending another celebration yesterday morning. I now have the good fortune to attend the blessed sacrament every Sunday at 7 am, so you know that every Sunday morning I draw near to the Throne of Grace – it is comforting to know that some of my loved ones – even at the same hour, are also so near to the divine presence. The link in the chain is unbroken – 'tis a glorious thought.

In many days I have been without any letters from the dear ones at home – I expect the Easter holidays must have upset the mails.[19] But this morning I had such a jolly surprise – I turned out early with the Padre and we motored up to the old canal (so well known to me in the old days), to hold a service for a unit in the forward area. We had a glorious celebration. It brought back those old days of 1915, especially as the service was held in the old district I know so well. About 15 attended the service and afterwards we had breakfast in a priceless little dugout. After breakfast I visited the old cemetery and saw the graves of several of my comrades. I also saw the old barge in the canal[20]. I think that sketch of mine, which I did some time ago is now in the album in the drawing room. It was after we returned to the Squadron that I had the surprise – the mail had turned up and I had a splendid harvest of eight letters.

I was fearfully bucked and how I enjoyed reading all the welcome news. I am delighted to know that you all spent such a happy Easter and I am sure the Vicar would be delighted with the congregations. Just at this moment I can hear some lovely strains of Chopin coming from the mess. The pianist is an exquisite player – he plays my favourite pieces nearly every night.

I am sorry to hear that Cyril has been doing such an extraordinary thing. I hope he has

19 ... and the chaos of the retreat?
20 NOTE: The Yser Canal in the Ypres sector.. See page 25 for this sketch.

not damaged his foot seriously. I am sure the garden must be bucking up immensely and I am pleased the rockeries are looking so well. I am delighted to hear that the photos have arrived. How are the Debenham photos turning out? I hope they will send you some photo post-cards as well.

I am having this posted in England, so that I shall not cause any delay, as I know you expect my Sunday letter on a Thursday. Has Edward gone into his new ship yet? I am pleased he is better – I am writing him tonight. My office of P.M.C.[21] is causing me much labour but I am bored if I have nothing to do.

I don't think William and Murville are at present in the line, as I heard from William the other day. Well my dearest ones I have run out of news, so I will conclude now. My sincere thanks to you all for your welcome and loving letters. I commit you all unto the care of our heavenly Father and may He grant His blessings upon the home and keep you all in His loving care. With my fondest love and xx to you all.
Ever your loving Son

AGW

P.S. I would like you to acknowledge letters by the number then I can check them – 57 was the last I think.

---

21 P.M.C. – Perhaps President of the Mess Committee.

I conclude Jolly Pièrre's story of the War with:

Extracts From Diaries & Memoirs

9 April 1918

*S*udden early morning news of dramatic Hun attack on Armentières Front. Much excitement in Sqdn. Sent on special reconnaissance down south as I knew the area well from 1915.

10ᵗʰ April 1918
Up at 4 a.m. with Harland and I know village of our objective. Very dull morning, rain and fog. I direct Maurice and see many farms burning – spot Glenny in his machine and suddenly see him nose dive – I fear he is hit. We fly low over well-known area and get heavily shot at by Hun machine gunners. I manage to make contact with Worcesters by my lamp and klaxon. Then we were flying at 200-300 feet. Most important contact with Worcesters – amazing sight to witness French evacuation of Armentières. We return to Proven and just before landing see a landing RE8 blow up, as bombs explode. King and Hughes killed.

Habgood gives me excellent help with reports – ours the only machine to return from the initial six sent out to check German advance.[22]

Up again immediately with McClurg. We proceed South to bomb Merville. Fly over hordes of Huns on roads and they blaze away at us as we fly over. We bomb our old billet of W.Yorks of 1915. Flying low, I fire 400 rounds at masses of Hun troops. Whole countryside ablaze from Merville to Armentières. We land to find many machines missing, but to our joy Glenny turns up wearing a comic bowler hat. Inman and Gersen still missing and Lloyd Rey wounded and landed at St Omer. The French Staff arrive to take over Proven Aerodrome and I'm told we move to Droglandt tomorrow. Very busy packing up Mess. Morgan works admirably.

13ᵗʰ April 1916
Orders for move to Droglandt confirmed. Machines leave carrying dogs, kit, very many cases of whisky, goat and all our possessions. I follow with men, kit and Headquarters. Utter chaos on roads. Civilians wheeling their possessions and infants in prams and small carts.

15ᵗʰ April 1916
We soon located battle from fires everywhere and identified French troops from 500 ft, along Mont de Cars. Watch French Infantry attack German Trenches. Whole battle

---

22 It was for his vital work under heavy fire during the retreat, reporting where British and German units were, that he was awarded his MC.

front amazing sight, lines of French 75s in action, firing at point blank range at Huns. French Gunners in bare chests loading 75s – terribly fast and causing tremendous havoc in German lines. Saw French Infantry capture German Trenches. We flew backwards and forwards along battle front at under 500'. It was clear the French had succeeded in halting the main German attack, and at this point, with the terrific support from the scores of French 75s, were inflicting immense casualties on the Huns. I watched this mighty battle for two hours and finally left for our return flight to Droglandt. On arriving back found Wright DCM and Coombes missing somewhere near Merville. Now snowing and roads in a frightful mess. All in favour of the wretched Hun. Retired to my hut early as I was very exhausted. Huns bomb us every night.

26th April 1918
We had a big dinner party and entertained lots of French Air Aces, including George Guynemer, who introduced himself to each of the Sqdn as follows: He stood erect in front of each of us and repeated his slogan, "Et moi, Guynemer, Chevalier Legion d'Honneur, Medaille Militaire, Croix de Guèrre quatre palmes" to each of us, saluting each member before his oration![23]

By the end of the evening almost all our French guests had "passed out" and at midnight we saw them to their cars.

28th April 1918
Fletcher and I were detailed to visit St Marie Capelle aerodrome, to which we were going to retreat. We were NOT impressed, as no place for mess, no huts for sleeping quarters; only big hangars with few huts as stores. We met Col. Barratt in St Omer and gave him our report. He was most unsympathetic and told us it would have to do. We could sleep in hangars and take our meals there.

30th April 1918
Our Sqdn. Commander, Sqdn. Ldr. B. E. Sutton D.S.O. M.C., calls on me early in my hut with most exciting news. He tells me, "Peter you have been awarded the M.C. and here is a copy of the thrilling signal." It was a copy of Army Orders by General Sir Herbert Plumber, Commanding the 2nd Army.

"Military Secretary's Branch, IMMEDIATE AWARDS Under authority delegated by His Majesty the King, the Field Marshal Commanding-in-Chief has made the following awards for gallantry and devotion to duty in action.

"The Military Cross to Lieut. A. G. Wilson, West Yorkshire Regiment, attd. Royal Air Force."

There were 12 names awarded the M.C. for gallantry during the recent German push.
23 My father's writing was tricky to read particularly regarding place names and surnames. Lyn Macdonald informed me that it could be Guynemer. If not Nungesser.

Imagine my thrill at this exciting news. The CO orders a Mark 1 for tonight, so I go off shopping to Dunkirk. Leete comes to help me buy wines, fish and other special foods. Eighty for dinner, including some French pilots. A terrific night in mess and Padré grants me a dispensation for Binge! I should mention here that I had been almost TT since August 1914, only permitting myself a small port when toasting the King's Health.

COPY OF TELEGRAM
FROM: GENERAL SIR DOUGLAS HAIG C/I/CHIEF B.E.F.
TO: OFFICER COMMANDING 7 SQUADRON R.A.F. 30 APL. 1918

UNDER AUTHORITY GRANTED BY H. M. THE KING COMMANDER IN CHIEF AWARDS MILITARY CROSS – LIEUT. A. G. WILSON WEST YORKS. REGT. FROM 2ND. WING. R.A.F.

TIME   07.30AM

COPY OF LONDON GAZETTE.   AWARD OF MILITARY CROSS.
LIEUT. A. G. WILSON 5TH. WEST YORKS. REGT. ATTCH. R. F. C.
"FOR CONSPICUOUS GALLANTRY AND DEVOTION TO DUTY. HE FLEW UNDER MOST DIFFICULT WEATHER CONDITIONS AND OBTAINED UNDER HEAVY FIRE, VALUABLE INFORMATION WHICH HE EMBODIED IN A SERIES OF EXCELLENT REPORTS. ON ONE OCCASION, WHEN A SMOKE SCREEN WAS PUT UP BY THE ENEMY, HE FLEW ROUND AND MADE A CLOSE RECONNAISSANCE FROM BETWEEN 500 TO 1000 FEET UNDER HEAVY ANTIAIRCRAFT AND MACHINE-GUN FIRE."

Wattie comes into dinner plastered with ribbon – a leg pull on Guynemer, the French Ace – he causes a sensation with the French Officers. Facey brings 20 double whiskies to me and orders me to drink all. I am Mess President and kept control of my alcoholic intake and went through dinner successfully – the noise is colossal. The Wing M.O. lifts me on to the top of the piano and I make many speeches.

June 1918
Up on dawn patrol with Facey. Huns put bullet through my camera tube. We finish patrol and I wireless Corps Hqrs. As Fletcher "Takes off", he unfortunately crashes straight into line of 5 RE8s and plays havoc with the rigging. Poor Harrison, his observer, looks very worried. We go to Czerney with Fletcher and Darnley to collect two more RE8s to replace yesterday's disaster. When flying the machines back to Droglandt they meet a storm and get lost – both machines crashing – one in midst of a battery and the second in a cabbage field.

Busy flying all June. CAP patrols. Photography and shoots against 6 Hun artillery batteries. Excellent results. Take photos of shots and visit Gunners with photos to show them results of their shoots – most satisfactory. Meet Sqdn. Ldr. Mannock V.C., D.S.O., M.C. He lunches with us. Most delightful chap, he has already shot down 54 Huns. He is killed the next week. This is really what he wanted[24], so he told me, as he had seen many of his victims shot down in flames. He has memorial in Canterbury Cathedral.

15th June 1918
On Counter Attack Patrol with Allanson over Ypres Front. Up at 2.30 am with Facey. We take off in darkness and fly over Ypres and drop special flares on Hun working parties. Alarming sight from back seat of RE8..

REX FACEY'S LOG BOOK

By a happy coincidence (August 2007) I have just come across Rex Facey's Pilot's Flying Log Book which clearly shows a 2.40 am take-off, with Wilson as Observer, on June 16th, 1918.

16th June 1918
My friend at No 10 Sqdn., Coomb-Taylor, killed in crash. Was his guest at No. 10 Sqdn. only last night

24 I understand that this syndrome affected several aces on both sides.

18th June 1918

As we are all enjoying lunch, an Orderly arrives with special message from Corps Headquarters. Bertie reads it and taking a pen, writes on the form and looks at me grinning all over his face. He hands the form to me to read and it says, "Arrange for lecture to the American Corps School." Bertie's reply written on form states "Lt. Wilson will lecture American School at Merckegheim."
I am very surprised, windy and irritated by this sudden act.

19th - 20th June 1918

Very busy all day preparing lectures and arrange to leave early, as Merckegheim is a long journey right in the Belgian zone. "Subject of lecture: Artillery co-operation with Aircraft.*" Harper accompanies me and we arrive at No. 10 American Corps School. I am amazed at huge audience in large hall. Many senior officers present and large display of flowers. Hosts of Yanks produce note books and I proceed with my lecture for about 40 mins. Then long spell of discussion and questions for further half hour. I am entertained to dinner with US Staff, with excellent food and much wine. Finally, my driver arrives with Harper, who is very cheery. We leave for Droglandt at 10.30 pm. Long drive back, arrive 2 am.*

27th June 1918

Final flight with Rex Facey – but we have engine trouble, so I bid farewell to Ypres Salient area – so well known to me 1915-1918. Feel very sad I am leaving Sqdn. for Home Establishment.

An R.E.8 setting out on night flight

This photo of a night flight was amongst Peter's papers:
Printed courtesy of Imperial War Museum and shows an RE8 of
No. 69 Squadron Australian Flying Corps

ALBERT IN RUINS

*By August 1918, the tide of war was turning with terrible devastation
left in its wake as shown by this picture of the cathedral in
Albert just after its recapture by the British.*

And by contrast, I think that this poem, which I have recently found in my father's papers, most beautifully encapsulates the magical, almost mystical experience it must have been for those first warriors of the air to fly.

Man had only made the first flight a few years before.

> High in the sunlit silence, hovering there,
> I've chased the shouting wind along, and flung
> My eager craft through footless halls of air.
>
> Up, up the long delirious brimming blue,
> I've topped the windswept heights with easy grace,
> Where never lark nor even eagle flies,
> And, while with silent lifting mind I've trod,
> The high untrespassed sanctity of space,
> Put out my hand and touched the Face of God.

P.O. Magee

94

My father was posted to R.A.F. Reading (as the R.F.C. had become), as an Instructor on Observation and Artillery Co-operation.

It is fitting to end his story of the war by a note from his diary dated –

November 11th 1918

My leave ending, and due to return South in morning. At York by 10 am. Hear Armistice has been signed; the Minster Bells ring out in wonderful peal. Catch train for King's Cross. Met by Rex Facey. There is very much excitement. Station packed with Troops and excited civilians.

All London streets packed. Flags out everywhere. Rex and self join in crowds of excited folk. We walk down The Mall to join crowds at Buckingham Palace – never seen so much excitement. Thousands round the railings at Buckingham Palace. King and Queen received tremendous reception from the Balcony – they put in several appearances. It is dark when we return to the Strand to find traffic congestion and excited crowds everywhere.

Trafalgar Square incredible sight – crowds jump in the water sections and climb the lions. Buses and taxis crowded with passengers and make very slow progress down Strand. We manage to get into restaurant for dinner and join in with party of eight – very funny, nobody knew each other. Three girls join in with us for celebration dinner. By 8 pm many very cheery folk, both sexes and our waiter is excellent. The restaurant put on a splendid dinner, we enjoy good wines and the dinner goes on for a couple of hours. Outside in the Strand the whole street is crowded and buses simply cannot move. Rex and I collect two of the very attractive girls from dinner and join in with the rejoicing crowds, who ramble aimlessly up and down the Strand and round Trafalgar Square.

Many in the crowds were heavily intoxicated but no sordid scenes. Several friendly types offered us drink from bottles of wine. Some hearties had produced some fireworks in Trafalgar Square. We decided that by midnight we had had enough and said au revoir to the two charming girls, who seemed sad to say farewell. Rex took me to his home in Harrington Gardens for the night and we finally retired at 2 am.

*Peter and friends, now R.A.F. with a Bristol Fighter of 9 Squadron
at Mulheim with the British Army of the Rhine in 1919*

Epilogue

I think it is not surprising that my father was nicknamed "Jolly Pièrre" by his companions in arms. His resilience, his courageous optimism and his sense of fun must have played an important part in maintaining morale, even if it could be a bit "over the top" at times!

My dear old Dad seemed to bear a charmed life, what with shells, snipers and aircraft crashes. I think the fact that he was a small man, about 5'6", probably saved him from those deadly snipers.

I find these letters, and the glimpses they give us of what those young soldiers had to endure, a remarkable testimony of how the human spirit can triumph over adversity. In my father's case his Christian Faith played a huge part in maintaining his steadfast hope in the future. You will not be surprised to learn that he and his sister Barbara contemplated becoming missionaries in Africa after the war.

Readers may wonder what became of the dear man. Well: he volunteered for the Army of Occupation (RAF) in Germany in 1919. While there he responded to the sense of calling he felt when in the trenches and decided he would like to become a doctor. He was encouraged by his old pilot, Rex Facey, to join him at Brasenose College, Oxford, to read medicine.

He enjoyed three happy years at Oxford, mixing easily with veterans and with "Freshers" straight from school. To the latter, battle scarred, decorated and some seven years older, he must have had quite an aura! He continued to enjoy his rugby.

Then in 1923, aged 28, he was accepted by St Thomas's Hospital to complete his training as a doctor, becoming M.R.C.S., L.R.C.P. in1926. He then joined a practice in Radlett, Hertfordshire as a G.P.

While at St Thomas's, my father fell in love with a nurse, Sheena Allan, twelve years his junior. They were married in September 1927. Sadly they were not compatible and separated in 1932 shortly after my sister, Fiona, was born.

No sooner was the devastating recession overcome in the early thirties, than a new, menacing shadow was cast over Europe. Hitler and his cronies threatened the peace which had been purchased with so much toil and sacrifice.

Peter's response was to volunteer for the R.A.F.V.R., and so it was that in September 1939 he was mobilised as an R.A.F doctor. It was his proud boast that he had served his country in both World Wars, from the first day till the last. Peter's old Squadron Leader, Bertie Sutton, now an Air Vice Marshall, insisted that he join Training Command at Cranwell, where his WW1 experience with the RFC was invaluable. Having started the

War as a Flying Officer, he ended it as a Wing Commander and S.M.O. (Senior Medical Officer) of a Group, via interludes with Fighter and Bomber Commands.

He was demobbed in 1945, a very fit 50 year old, and returned to General Practice in Radlett, a much loved if rather lonely "Doc".

In 1961 after a long and companionable courtship, my father married again. His wife, Paula, also a medical person twelve years his junior, cared for him until 1984, when she predeceased him by 6 years.

He retired in 1966, but his partners allowed him to work part time until 1974, when, after nearly 48 years caring for the people of Radlett, he and Paula moved to Rockbourne, near Salisbury.

The story of Peter's life would not be complete without a mention of his recreational passions. Shooting, he was an excellent shot; fishing, he was a wily and persistent fisherman (his Game Book records 600 salmon); and gardening. His gardens in Radlett, and in Rockbourne, were his pride and joy and a delight to behold. These three hobbies kept him a fulfilled and happy man from 1932 to 1961, when Paula joined him, and indeed long into retirement. He had wonderful and generous friends who loved his company and he never once had to pay for a day's sport.

Mention should also be made of the huge enjoyment he and Paula got from four long visits to Brazil (where I was based), to which we treated them in his eighties. When he first spied the glorious constellation of the Southern Cross in the heavens, he nearly levitated with excitement!

And so in April 1990, at the ripe old age of 95, this gallant soldier and airman, this enthusiastic sportsman, this dedicated Doc, this skilful gardener, this lively raconteur and beloved grandfather, was finally laid to rest.

This little book would never have been written had not those special letters from Flanders in 1915, been discovered languishing in a Maida Vale Police Station. I have felt in duty bound to share them with family and friends and maybe, a slightly wider audience. Ninety years on they remind us what horrendous conditions men fought and died in, and what huge sacrifices the men and their families were called upon to make. Sadly mankind has not learned the lessons history should teach. They also gave clear evidence of the special man emerging from the trials and tribulations of Flanders. I would be so pleased if some readers found their own faith rekindled by Peter's stalwart trust in his Heavenly Father.

After his death we received many glowing tributes, and in closing Peter's story may I share a few, showing how he had touched the lives of different people in different ways:

"A rich and full life lived with courage and panache"
"A trusted and valued confidant in time of trouble"
"... loving care and tenderness"
"... cannot think that he ever did, or even thought, a mean act";

and memories of his trilling whistled signature tune and gorgeous buttonholes, as he visited the sick and happily dispensed his gift of "making people happy", and feel better, even if they were not.

Or again –

"Trembling with excitement long before the grouse flew over."

And I particularly cherish this memory of an old friend,

"After he had taken his communion, he would come back to all of us and somehow enfold us all with his love and affection and fun."

As for me, my quiverful of memories spans nearly six decades – before the war: the zoo, great fun with elephants and baboons; splendid sessions at those delightful Silly Symphony and Mickey Mouse movies (we usually sat through the whole programme twice!); visiting patients. During the war: visions of air bases; two wangled flights in Training Command planes, and poaching pheasants and partridges; his interminable sermon in the Yorkshire Dales.

Later on: visits to me at Brasenose, fishing and shooting holidays in the Highlands during which, after dinner, he would keep the whole party enthralled with his yarns; gardening at Grove House, concerts; theatres. And latterly some wonderful long visits to us in Brazil, where his octogenarian enthusiasm led to invitations to give talks about gardens, flowers and the stars.

And one of my last memories of him, who was "game to the end", in hospital bestowing an enchanting Puckish smile upon one of his marvellous nurses.

And so, my dear old Dad, Au Revoir. I hope to see you soon.

Michael A Wilson
High Auchensail Farmhouse,
CARDROSS, Argyll & Bute.
G82 5HN

January 2008   ©

PETER'S MEDALS

Worn with pride on many occasions as you can see below.

WORLD WAR I:

Military Cross 30.4.18	1914-15 Star	1914-1918 British War Medal	1914-1919 Victory Medal

WORLD WAR II

Defence Medal 1939-1945	Victory Medal 1939-1945		Air Efficiency Award

*Peter and his parents leave Buckingham Palace after he was presented
with his decoration by the King*

Peter ready for the Remembrance Sunday Parade when over 90.

Michael and family visit Peter and Paula when on leave from Brazil 1971.

I will leave you with these words given to Peter by a friend in the trenches in 1915:

"I would be true for there are those who trust me,
I would be pure for there are those who care,
I would be strong for there is much to suffer,
I would be brave for there is much to dare,
I would be friend to all – the foe – the friendless,
I would be giving and forget the gift,
I would be humble for I know my weakness,
I would look up – and laugh
                – and love
                – and live."

Howard Arnold Natters

Peter on Armistice Sunday 1988.

This book has been compiled and edited by Peter Wilson's son, Michael. Born in 1928, after serving in the Navy, he followed his father to Brasenose College, Oxford, where he read Geology. He then joined J & P Coats, later Coats Patons, with whom he had a fulfilling career in marketing for 35 years – mainly based in South America - Cuba, Colombia, Chile and Brazil. His four sons were all born in South America after his marriage to Rosemary in 1958. The whole family is deeply attached to that wonderful continent and its people. They have had fun exploring remote areas like the Amazon, Pantanal and the Andes. He is now retired in the West of Scotland and has been busy creating a wild garden from a derelict wood, hill-walking with friends and doing sundry local activities in the community where he lives.

Michael Wilson

If you would like to find out more about the wonderful work being done by Combat Stress and Erskine for our ex-Servicemen and women, their details are as follows:

COMBAT STRESS: www.combatstress.org.uk
Address: Tyrwhitt House, Oaklawn Road, Leatherhead, Surrey KT22 OBX
Telephone: 01372 841600

ERSKINE: www.erskine.org.uk
Address: Erskine, Bishopton, Renfrewshire PA7 5PU
Telephone: 0141 812 1100